Navigating the Waves of Grief

"*Navigating the Waves of Grief* is a beautifully structured, deeply compassionate guide through the disorienting landscape of grief. With emotional depth, spiritual sensitivity, and grounded practices, Meyer invites readers to explore their inner world with honesty, gentleness, and care. A meaningful and compassionate resource for those seeking both reflection and relief, especially beyond easy answers often asked of grievers after loss."

—**Gina Moffa, LCSW**, author of
Moving On Doesn't Mean Letting Go

"I applaud all the loving and carefully written exercises for healing from grief that Kate put into each section of *Navigating the Waves of Grief*. As a therapist myself, clients are often looking for concrete things they can do to feel better, and these tools will be helpful for both the clients and their therapists. The exercises and the stages reflect her thoughtfulness and extensive experience as both an ordained minister and as a licensed professional counselor."

—**Rev. Dr. Pamela Pater-Ennis, LCSW, MDiv, PhD**,
founder and CEO of Hudson River Care and Counseling
and My Sanctuary Healing, Inc.

"I began working with Kate after the sudden loss of my brother—one of the closest people in my life. The tools in this book are the very ones that helped me navigate that overwhelming season, and they continue to support me today. As a therapist and grief companion, I've shared Kate's work with countless clients, and I'm so grateful to now have this book to recommend not only to clients, but also to friends, family, and anyone living with loss. It's a compassionate, flexible, and deeply healing resource for the ongoing journey of grief."

—**Lora Grabow, LMSW**, therapist and grief companion

"*Navigating the Waves of Grief* is a compassionate and practical guide for navigating loss and grief. With heartfelt wisdom and opportunities for reflective processing, it offers genuine comfort and instills hope. Whether you're grieving or supporting someone who is, its honesty makes it a must-read companion through one of life's most challenging seasons."

—**Dr. Catherine Mueller-Bell, LPC, PhD**, director of Mapalo Counseling Ministries, professor of clinical mental health counseling

"Kate Meyer has done it again. Using evocative wave imagery, *Navigating the Waves of Grief*, offers a compelling, comforting companion that takes readers on a journey of ebb and flow, at once deeply personal and a reminder that we are not alone. It is spiritually hospitable and welcoming, with a multi-layered, easy-to-engage format that includes generous reflection sections and gentle calls to action. Whether read as a continuation of *Faith Doesn't Erase Grief* or as a stand-alone, *Navigating the Waves of Grief* is an indispensable resource for anyone seeking to move forward in healthy, healing ways."

—**Rev. Elizabeth Testa, MDiv**, director of Equity-Based Hospitality and Women's Transformation + Leadership, Reformed Church of America

Navigating the Waves of Grief

Healing Prompts & Reflections to Move You Forward

Kate J. Meyer, MDiv, LPC

lakedrivebooks.com

Lake Drive Books
6757 Cascade Road SE, #162
Grand Rapids, MI 49546

info@lakedrivebooks.com
lakedrivebooks.com
@lakedrivebooks

Publishing books that help you heal, grow, and discover.

Copyright © 2025 by Kate J. Meyer

All rights reserved, including the right to reproduce this book or portions thereof in any format whatsoever. No part of this publication may be reproduced or transmitted in any form or by any means, electronic or mechanical, including photocopying, recording, or any other information storage and retrieval methods, without the written permission of the publisher.

Scripture quotations marked NRSV are taken from the New Revised Standard Version Bible. Copyright © 1989 National Council of the Churches of Christ in the United States of America. Used by permission. All rights reserved worldwide.

Scripture quotations marked NLT are taken from the Holy Bible, New Living Translation. Copyright © 1996, 2004, 2015 by Tyndale House Foundation. Used by permission of Tyndale House Ministries, Carol Stream, Illinois 60188. All rights reserved.

Scripture quotations marked MSG are taken from The Message, copyright © 1993, 2002, 2018 by Eugene H. Peterson. Used by permission of NavPress. All rights reserved. Represented by Tyndale House Publishers.

Paperback ISBN: 978-1-957687-68-1
E-book ISBN: 978-1-957687-69-8
Library of Congress Control Number: 2025906542

Cover design by Michael J. Williams

This book is not intended as a substitute for the medical advice of physicians or mental health professionals. The reader should consult a physician or mental health professional in matters relating to health and particularly with respect to any symptoms that may require diagnosis or medical attention. If you are feeling suicidal, thinking about hurting yourself, or are concerned that someone you know may be in danger of hurting himself or herself, call the National Suicide Prevention Lifeline at 1-800-273-TALK (1-800-273-8255). You can also find help in locating a mental health professional by consulting with your health care provider.

Contents

Introduction   1

1. Emotions   13
2. Connection   65
3. Identity   113
4. Through   161

   Now What?   209
   About the Author   211

Introduction

As I went through my new computer, freshly loaded with transferred content, I stumbled upon an audio file long forgotten. Knowing that my extended family would also enjoy hearing Grandpa's voice again, I decided to listen to it before emailing it out in case anything needed further explanation. I settled in, heart prepared to hear Grandpa read a story, and pressed play. I had closed my eyes to take in the experience, but seconds after I pressed play, my eyes flew open. My heart rate skyrocketed as *Grandma's* voice filled the room. Here was a wave of emotion that I didn't see coming. I had completely forgotten her introduction of the story and was not prepared to hear her voice. At all. The tears poured out before I could process what was happening. I paused the file to ground myself before restarting it and receiving the love of Grandpa and Grandma.

If you are reading these words, it is safe to say that you are familiar with grief and its accompanying, sometimes unpredictable waves like the one I experienced. Grief waves are inevitable, and they do not adhere to a predictable, convenient schedule. However, grief waves can lessen over time in duration, frequency, and intensity if you are willing to put in the work.

The tools in this book will help you to process the layers of your changed reality and release the emotions that might otherwise keep you trapped in this season of grief so that you can move forward as a changed person. Death and other losses change us, yet if we accept that fact and embrace the change process, we can heal and reengage with life. I am proud of you for taking this important step in your healing.

The Elephant in the Room

The common classification for this type of resource is "devotional journal," but those words are weighted with many interpretations and, for some, might serve as a barrier. To assuage any possible concerns you might have in that regard, let's get a few details out of the way.

First, though written specifically with Christian grievers in mind, this book is easily adapted for those who believe in Jesus but not the church—welcome, deconstructers!—those who believe in another divine reality, or for those who are broadly spiritual. As I state in my previous book *Faith Doesn't Erase Grief*, faith is meant to assist us in processing grief, not to impede it. Second, the word "devotional" carries with it a certain connotation and expected formula, and yes, I make occasional biblical references, but the goal of this work is to help grievers walk through to the other side of grief. Period. There is no preconceived end goal, or starting place for that matter, related to if or how your faith is used or impacted by engaging this work. I do encourage people to set goals for their faith (perhaps you want to maintain, pause, dig deeper, or explore), but I do not prescribe a goal because that decision is personal. No one—not me, not a pastor or faith leader, not a trusted friend, not even a therapist—has the right to set that goal for you. That is for you alone.

Third, if you read *Faith Doesn't Erase Grief*, you know I encourage a variety of journal writing techniques along with other forms of creative expression, but if you are not a "Dear Diary" person, fear not. Even the pages with prompts can be completed without writing. Try. Just try it. I believe you will be pleasantly surprised at the outcome.

Is This Tool for Me?

If you selected this book seeking help working through your grief, the simple answer to this question is an unequivocal "yes!" For those who need a bit more assurance than that, I'll offer this. *Navigating the Waves of Grief* is for grievers, whether that grief is the result of death (human or animal) or another kind of loss. Loss tugs at the heart; it upends what is and causes disorientation before you can find stability in your new reality. For the remainder of the book, I will reference grief as caused by death, but if the source of your grief is not death, know that you can still benefit from this work.

What If My Grief Is Not the Result of a Loving Relationship?

Yes, grief does still follow the death of a person with whom you had a strained, broken, estranged, or unfulfilled relationship. This is the case for adoptees whose birth parent died before they could meet, for those whose parent abandoned them emotionally, mentally, or physically, for those who were betrayed by friends, and many other similar relationship scenarios.. Despite the reality of this kind of pain, when they were alive, there remained a hope, no matter how small, of reconciliation and forgiveness. You might be grieving the person they never were or the person they became, yet you are still grieving. This guidebook will help you navigate those waves of grief too. Keep going; this tool is for you.

What If It's Been a Year or More?

I want to be clear about this from the outset: You do not need to be within the first year since the death to use this guidebook. No matter how long it has been since the death, if an old grief is reawakened, never went away, or is related to another type of loss, this guidebook is for you.

How to Use This Book

As with *Faith Doesn't Erase Grief*, *Navigating the Waves of Grief* breaks the mold of similar books, so I'll take a moment to explain how I've designed this book to work. First of all, grief is far too unpredictable for you to proceed through this book from beginning to end, so when you sit down with it—we'll discuss frequency in a moment—go to the section that best fits the moment. You might move within all four sections in a week, or you might complete one section before moving to the next, but the *how* does not matter. The only thing you need to do is show up and do the work.

Second, this book is composed of four sections that correspond to different aspects of grief work: Emotions, Connection, Identity, and Through. These are not stages or phases of grief, but aspects or features of grief that you'll experience in most of its phases. Each section has its own introduction that provides a more in-depth explanation of what it covers and when focusing on that aspect of grief might be most useful. For now, know that whenever you pick up this book, you can turn to whichever theme you prefer, but before you begin a section, read through its introduction.

Third, this resource is designed to be used in the moment, in preemptive preparation, or to help you find solid ground after a wave knocks you down. You can use it every day or as needed, whatever frequency you need. In addition, you may find there are stretches of time when the grief waters are calm and, especially the further out from the death you are, blissfully free of waves. Sometimes a break from grief work is needed. Go at the pace your grief needs: nothing more, nothing less.

Fourth, Toolkit pages and Reflection pages (here are my replacement words for "devotional" and "journal" pages, respectively) are scattered throughout the four sections of this guidebook; there is a combined total of twenty-five per section. You will not find the first half of the book to be only Reflections and the latter half only the more practical Toolkits. This is intentional. It reflects the changing needs of grief—where the work is always a combination of thought and actions—and allows this to be a more versatile tool. You choose whatever looks helpful each time you open the book. I'll keep saying it: Make this work for *your* grief.

Fifth, there are a few Toolkits that repeat throughout this guide:

- **Object Lesson.** This is the first Toolkit in each section and is meant to capture the way your grief changes as you do the work. I encourage you to complete one of these as your *first* activity to capture how your grief feels on the day you start this work. The other three Object Lessons can be completed at any time.
- **Guided Free Association.** This is a tool to help you discover emotions and thoughts you cannot access or are avoiding. It is in each section, but the suggested focus changes slightly depending on the section's theme. You may complete these in any order.
- **Horizon Line.** You will find this activity in sections two through four, and it is meant to help you focus on what is ahead. Again, you can complete these in any order.
- **Trajectory Tracker.** You will find one of these at the end of each section. You can elect to complete them at random or reserve them for when you finish a section,

but do not save them all for the end. Similar to the Object Lesson Toolkit, the Trajectory Tracker Toolkit is another way to help you visualize your forward movement through grief; therefore, spacing these out over time will increase their benefit.

Sixth, each thought-provoking Reflection ends with a simple Action Challenge related to the Reflection. Most challenges are intended to be completed in the moment, though there are a few that you'll be asked to complete on a different timeline. For those challenges, I encourage you to set a reminder in your calendar to come back to the page and record the outcome. Additionally, a few Reflections include a Next Level challenge beyond the action challenge. You choose when and whether to complete that challenge.

Finally, because this book will likely stir up a lot of feelings and insights, it might be challenging at times. I encourage you to reach out to a therapist or trusted friend to further discuss and process what rises to the surface. One of the both/and truths of grief is that it is meant to be experienced both alone and with others. *Navigating the Waves of Grief* can be a starting place to experience grief both alone and with others, if you're willing. Regardless of how you implement it, this book is designed to be an anchor to prevent you from capsizing in the waves. In these pages I trust you will find what you need to take command of these inevitable waves of grief.

Faith Doesn't Erase Grief: The Basics

I wrote *Faith Doesn't Erase Grief* for all the grievers who are also believers who arrived at my office for bereavement counseling burdened not only by their grief but also by the weight of shame or guilt heaped upon them by their pastor or another leader in their church. Session after session, I witnessed clients wrestle with wanting to—needing to—grieve while being pressured at every turn to simply rejoice that the person who died is now in heaven. "I'M STILL HERE!" was the refrain from each client. "Yes, they are in heaven, but I'm left to do life without them." Some clients went a step further, adding, "And I don't want to rejoice. I'm not okay with their death, and I'm certainly not ready to rejoice." Grievers who are religious often feel this way because faith truly cannot erase the human, natural experience we call grief. *Faith Doesn't Erase Grief* was written in honor of all those clients longing to both grieve and believe.

It is not necessary to have read *Faith Doesn't Erase Grief* for this guidebook to be useful, though you will notice that the Reflection pages and most Toolkit pages include quotes from *Faith Doesn't Erase Grief*, so you will get a sampling of that book as you work through this guidebook. *Faith Doesn't Erase Grief* paints in broad strokes with primarily an abstract, informational purpose, whereas this guidebook provides practical tools and personal interaction that apply specific teachings from *Faith Doesn't Erase Grief*. The first book is passive and reflective; this book is active and instructive.

Because the two books do go hand in hand, though, there are a few basics that are worth reviewing before you work through the sections ahead. The most important piece of information I want you to know from *Faith Doesn't Erase Grief* is about the grief process. Many models of grief exist, and there are things to be learned from each of those models; however, I find that they are generally too prescriptive. For this reason, I propose a more phasic approach to grief, breaking the grief trajectory down into Early Grief, Middle Grief, and Lasting Grief, each of which are referenced throughout this resource.

These phases are fluid, meaning grievers might find themselves straddling two phases at once, and as concepts they are meant not to direct what you do with your grief but to help you locate yourself within grief. Each phase, discussed next, is defined in part by a range of time, but it is important to note that those timelines are most relevant only for those experiencing grief without trauma. If there is any reason you were unable to begin grieving immediately following a death (as can happen with trauma), these timelines might feel off. If this is the case for you, consider when you were able to start grieving—perhaps the court case ended, your person was found, or the results came in—and set that as your day one. Doing so might help the timelines of each phase feel like a better fit.

Early Grief begins the moment of the person's death (or the moment you first truly registered the loss) and can last anywhere up to five months. It is the time when grief is raw, you feel numb, and there is no escaping the weight of it. It is a constant companion that cannot be outrun. This is the phase when people describe feeling like a different person or disconnected or uncomfortable in their own skin. It's all too much too fast. It is also the phase in which grievers live mostly in the past with very little thought of the present, and the idea of the future is laughable. The body takes on new pains, the brain doesn't function well, and emotions are unpredictable. In short, Early Grief is about daily survival. Complete the needs of the day, and if that's all you can do, that's okay. The rest will still be there tomorrow.

Middle Grief is the marathon phase, beginning as early as month two and lasting up to month ten, but there is good news: In this phase, grievers begin to experience things that are more comfortable. Laughter, smiles, reconnecting with friends and family, and hope all begin to creep back in. As difficult as these are to find and genuinely experience in Early Grief, in Middle Grief the experience shifts. It is in Middle Grief that grievers begin fully accepting and integrating the death into their daily lives. They live more in the present and eventually begin to consider the future. They find that fatigue lessens, the brain fog clears, and tolerance of others increases. Middle Grief is the "doing" phase, and it is filled with opportunity.

As for Lasting Grief, I struggled with naming this third phase because I needed a word that captured the fact that grief doesn't truly end. It changes in the impact it has and in the level of intrusion into your daily life, but you don't stop grieving; you don't just stop missing the person who died. I settled on *lasting* because it reflected those realities while also feeling gentler than saying, "You're never done." Grievers can transition into Lasting Grief as early as month eight, though some do not reach it until after the first year. This phase is marked with a full acceptance of the death and a complete return to engagement in life. The griever has learned who they are now and knows the direction they are heading. They can remember the person with more joy (or at least closure) than pain, and they can share memories with gratitude or at least a sense of peace. It's a time of hope, direction, and purpose. A time when grief shifts from being a person's whole identity to just an aspect of it.

Beyond these proposed phases of grief, there are two additional concepts taught in *Faith Doesn't Erase Grief* that I will explain here so that you feel prepared when you come upon them as you work through the pages ahead. The first is the concept of a continued albeit changed relationship with the person who died. I regularly use the phrase "physical presence" throughout this guidebook as a reminder that though their physical presence is gone from this world, many other aspects of them remain. It is these pieces of your person that you choose to connect with, to whatever degree. A continued connection is not necessary to move through grief, but it can help. Take your time with this concept if it is new to you and allow it to unfold in the pages ahead as you come across it. You do not need to make any decisions right now. Just know the concept is included and be prepared to interact with it however you see fit.

The second concept to understand is that there is no moving on; there is only moving forward. The word "on" carries a connotation of leaving something behind or closing a book.

That is not the goal of grief work. The goal of grief work is to adapt to your loss and integrate it into your whole sense of self so that you can continue living, even carrying your person into the future with you, if that makes sense to you. The grief no longer dominates your life, but it remains, and moving forward represents living in that adjusted reality.

Finally, it was not my goal or intention in *Faith Doesn't Erase Grief* to tell you what or how to grieve, nor is that my intention here. As a therapist, my job is to walk alongside you, point out what you might miss, help you consider additional perspectives, and empower you to take control in ways that work for you, your faith, and your grief. If something in this guidebook or in *Faith Doesn't Erase Grief* doesn't fit you, leave it. That's okay. Just like in therapy, it will only benefit you if it resonates. All I ask is for you to try.

I cannot do this work for you. No one can. I can, however, through this guidebook, help you along the way. Are you ready?

Your Power over the Waves of Grief

When the disciples stepped into the boat with Jesus that day, there was no indication of a brewing storm. I imagine that before it hit, those on the boat were catching up on things not related to the teacher, using the time he napped to take their own breaks. Then, suddenly, light became dark. Calm became panic. Peace became fear. Flat water became foaming, roaring waves. I envision the disciples scattering throughout the boat, trying to stay upright while also working to prevent capsizing, their bodies overwrought with fear, anxiety, and uncertainty. And all the while, Jesus slept.

Whether out of sheer disbelief and frustration that he was still asleep and *not helping* or because they suddenly realized he could do something they could not, Christ's followers finally woke him. At last, Jesus stood and commanded stillness. And the waves? They obeyed.

The initial reactions of grievers are often similar to those exhibited by the disciples when the storm first appeared. The sudden rush of emotion is enough to uproot us and fill us with dread. We try everything we know to find our bearings and gain solid ground, yet nothing works. The longer we go without relief, the more power the waves appear to have. Here's the truth we all need to hold: Just as the disciples had with them the one who could calm the storm, so you have within you the ability to command the waves of grief. Waves seem to have all the power, but they do not hold absolute power.

Will you ever learn to stop grief waves altogether? No. There are far too many variables outside your control. You can, however, limit the impact. *Navigating the Waves of Grief* is a training manual to do just that.

Emotions

God implanted humans with emotions to assist us in recognizing our own reactions to people, places, events, situations, memories, and more. Unfortunately, many adults are significantly out of touch with their emotions to the point that they are unable to define them, and if a person cannot put words to their emotions, then those emotions cannot be released. That might not sound like a problem, but trapped emotions keep a person stuck in grief, unable to make progress, detached from others, themselves, and God; they can even present as physical symptoms.

If emotions are not identified, expressed, and released, a person will still be able to make forward progress in some areas of grief, but never all areas. In other words, healing—that is, integrating the fullness of the loss and reengaging in life—cannot occur without acknowledging the full spectrum of emotions, both those that are comfortable to experience along with those that are uncomfortable and cause disruption.

I recognize that sounds like the opposite of fun, and I will not pretend this section will always be enjoyable, but what I can promise is that the unburdening of self from those uncomfortable emotions is akin to something better than fun: contentment, peace, acceptance, and stability.

In this section, each Toolkit and Reflection page is tied to identifying, processing, expressing, and/or releasing emotions commonly experienced in grief. Some pages suggest activities around a specific emotion, but you can focus on whatever emotion is most relevant to you at the time. Emotions are much more nuanced than the standard notions of happy, sad, or angry, so to best release an emotion, it is necessary to identify it as specifically as possible. Because of that, and because many of us do not know what names to give the emotions we feel, this section begins with an alphabetical Emotions List. If you do not know how to describe what you feel, scan the list until something resonates.

As a reminder, you can progress through this section however you desire. Simply showing up to engage the topic matters much more than perfect execution of the exercises. Create the space in your life to give yourself this gift of intentional engagement, be gentle with yourself as you work through it, and stay open to what you might learn.

Emotions List

Abandoned	Bright	Cross
Aching	Buoyant	Cruel
Adament	Burdened	Crushed
Adequate		
Affectionate	Calm	Daring
Afraid	Capable	Dark
Airy	Caring	Deceitful
Alarmed	Cautious	Defeated
Ambivalent	Challenged	Defiant
Angry	Cheated	Delighted
Annoyed	Cheerful	Depressed
Anxious	Cheerless	Despair
Apathetic	Childish	Destructive
Appalled	Choked up	Determined
Apprehensive	Clever	Different
Ashamed	Clouded	Diminished
Astounded	Combative	Disappointed
Awed	Comfortable	Discontented
	Competitive	Discouraged
Bad	Complacent	Dismal
Beautiful	Concerned	Dismayed
Betrayed	Condemned	Distracted
Bitter	Confident	Distraught
Blissful	Confused	Distressed
Boiling	Conspicuous	Distrustful
Bold	Contented	Disturbed
Bored	Contrite	Divided
Brave	Courageous	Dominated
Brisk	Cozy	Doubtful

Downcast	Flustered	Hesitant
Dreadful	Foolish	High
Dreary	Frantic	High-spirited
Dubious	Free	Homesick
Dull	Frightened	Honored
Dumb	Frisky	Hopeless
Dumped on	Frustrated	Horrible
	Full	Hurt
Eager	Fuming	Hysterical
Ecstatic	Furious	
Edgy		Ignored
Elated	Gallant	Immortal
Embarrassed	Glad	Impatient
Empty	Gloomy	Imposed upon
Encouraged	Glum	Impressed
Energetic	Grateful	Indecisive
Enraged	Gratified	Indignant
Enthusiastic	Greedy	Infatuated
Envious	Grief	Infuriated
Evasive	Grieved	Injured
Excited	Grumpy	Insecure
Evil	Guilty	Inspired
Exhausted	Gullible	Intimidated
Exhilarated		Intrigued
	Happy	Irate
Fainthearted	Hassled	Irritated
Fascinated	Hateful	Isolated
Fearful	Heartbroken	Itchy
Fearless	Heavyhearted	
Fidgety	Helpful	Jealous
Flat	Helpless	Jolly

Joyless	Obsessed	Restless
Joyous	Odd	Reverent
Jumpy	Offended	Rewarded
	Opposed	Righteous
Kind	Outraged	Run-down
	Overwhelmed	
Lazy		Sad
Left out	Painful	Satisfied
Lighthearted	Panicked	Saucy
Lively	Paralyzed	Scared
Lonely	Pathetic	Scattered
Lost	Peaceful	Secure
Loving	Persecuted	Serene
Low	Petrified	Settled
Lustful	Playful	Sexy
	Pleased	Shaky
Mad	Powerless	Shocked
Maudlin	Pressured	Silly
Mean	Pretty	Skeptical
Melancholy	Proud	Small
Miserable	Put down	Sneaky
Mixed-up		Soft
Moody	Quarrelsome	Solemn
Mournful		Somber
	Reassured	Sorrowful
Naughty	Refreshed	Sorry
Needed	Rejected	Sparkling
Nervous	Relaxed	Spiteful
Nice	Relieved	Startled
Nutty	Remorseful	Strange
	Resistant	Stringy

Strong
Stuffed
Stupid
Stunned
Sulky
Sullen
Sunny
Supported
Sure
Surprised
Sympathetic

Talkative
Tempted
Tender
Tense
Tentative
Terrible
Terrified
Thankful
Threatened
Timid
Tired
Torn
Tranquil
Trapped
Trembling
Troubled

Ugly
Uncertain
Uneasy
Unhappy
Unsettled
Uptight
Used

Vehement
Violent
Vivacious
Vulnerable

Warm
Wavering
Weak
Wicked
Wiped out
Woeful
Wonderful
Worked up
Worried
Worthless

TOOLKIT: OBJECT LESSON

If you had to illustrate your grief, what would it look like? The image that most resonates with me is that of a large internal ball with sharp edges that poke and prod, inflicting pain from head to toe when I move. Then, as I work at it, it slowly shrinks in size, and the spikes fall off. Draw what your grief looks like and how you carry it in your body. Is it all-consuming? Maybe it's on the smaller side, so that it bounces around your body? Are its edges sharp, dull, or some of each? Is it small enough that you can keep it in one place, tucked away where it causes minimal pain? Draw (or describe with words if that's more of your thing) what is true of you and your grief right now, and record the date.[1]

---

[1] This Toolkit repeats in each of the four main sections of this guidebook. Once you've completed one, reserve the completion of another until you become aware that your grief is different. Always include the date of completion so you have a concrete reminder that your grief has in fact changed.

Reflection

"The only way a person survives grief is to face it, and part of facing it means being brutally honest with expressing emotional truth."

Faith Doesn't Erase Grief, 17

I will forever remember the level of fatigue and the number of sore muscles that greeted me at the end of each day when I decided to repaint our entire kitchen—including the cabinets and counters! I spent many nights after work and whole weekends tackling the project, and at about the halfway mark, I was physically done. Over it. Unfortunately, by that point my cabinets were spread throughout my living room, half painted and half not, so stopping was not an option. I hadn't given up on what I wanted, but I was tired. My muscles weren't sore just at the end of the night; they hurt when I woke up in the morning, when I brushed my hair, when I bent down to pet the dog—basically from sunup to sundown—and that made it challenging to stay motivated. I wanted to soak in a hot tub, not do more work that was certain to cause more pain.

We are wired from a young age to turn away from pain, so much so that those of us who intentionally do things that cause pain (lift weights, get tattoos, etc.) often find ourselves on the receiving end of some interesting looks from others. While it is true this wiring to avoid pain serves us well in many situations, grief is a significant exception to that rule.

In grief, we must face and walk through the pain, even if each time we try to do so, our inner dialogue screams at us, "Stop! Hot! Don't touch!" Clearing this hurdle to force yourself to face the menagerie of emotions in grief is your primary emotional task. It's the one hurdle that you must jump for the rest to fall into place, and yet, as life tends to go, it is one of the most challenging to face.

Just as my perseverance paid off with a fresh, updated kitchen, there is a gift that awaits you each time you summon the courage to face your emotions and work to release them. It's not easy, and there will be days you don't want to. Don't aim for perfection. Just aim for more days when you allow yourself to face it than not.

Action Challenge

How can you stay motivated to face the pain and other emotions grief brings? Take a few moments to remember times in your life that you pushed through something difficult. What awaited you on the other side? Create a reminder for yourself of that experience to help you dig deep on the days you'd really rather not. You could attach with tape or write on a mirror a key word that helps you recall the example. Ask a friend to bring up the story when you need it most. Set a reminder on your phone. However you choose to do it, it will serve you well on those extra-challenging days.

TOOLKIT: RETURNING TO THE PRESENT

Because of the way the brain works, grief waves can be strong enough to trick your body into thinking you are reliving a situation from the dying process instead of simply remembering a past event from your place of safety in the present. Following is a mindfulness practice to help signal to your body that you are not back in the moment and that it is safe to relax. Why is this so important? A relaxed body cannot hold trauma. Learning how to remember the death without physiologically, emotionally, mentally, and spiritually re-experiencing the moment it happened will benefit your entire being as you weather a grief wave.

There are two different ways to do this, so I recommend trying both to see which is the best fit for you. Either can be completed on your own no matter where you are, either out loud or internally. If you're driving, it is obviously best to pull off the road to complete this exercise.

Option 1 (faster): Name five things that you see in your immediate surroundings, then four different things you hear, three different things you can touch, two different things you smell, and one thing you taste. Finally, tap your feet on the ground and state where you are and what you are doing. Note that the taste one can throw people off a bit, but it really does pull you further into the present to taste the mint or gum you might have in your mouth at the time or maybe the taste of your lip balm. Try not to overthink it.

Option 2 (a bit more complex): For round one, you will name three each of things you see, hear, touch, smell, and taste. For round two, name two of each, as many of them different from round one as you can find. End with a round naming one more of each, again different for as many as you're able.

When finished, tap your feet on the ground and state where you are and what you are doing. I recommend starting with three rounds for this, but you can start with two if that feels less intimidating. Just repeat the exercise if you do not feel fully grounded in the present when you finish the last round.

Reflection

"It can be tempting to study a map before starting on a hike. In the preparation you learn how long it might take, what you are going to need with you, and where you'll end up. That is a great plan for a true hike in the woods, but grief is different."
Faith Doesn't Erase Grief, 40

"I'm doing it again, aren't I?" my client asked. Though I already knew how I would answer her, I asked her to clarify. "I'm spending time preparing to have intentional grief time instead of actually taking time to intentionally grieve."

I smiled and nodded. This was a breakthrough for her, and I had asked for the clarification because I needed her to recognize her own growth. After all, in grief, every conceivable victory counts.

Emotional avoiders—people who consume so much self-help content just to ignore their own emotions, often while supporting others through *their* emotions—are masters of positive avoidance. They know the process of releasing emotions is important, so they invest their time and energy into learning how best to do so. Unfortunately, reading about the thing and doing the thing are not the same. To continue the analogy from the opening quote, positive avoidance would be studying the map, buying the shoes and the poles, and preparing a day pack, and then realizing you spent all the time you had for the hike on preparing for it rather than actually hiking. Listening to grief podcasts, reading all the latest books on grief and emotions, stocking up with a new journal and pen, and even helping others with their emotions are all meant to be *supplements* to grief work, not replacements of it.

Grief is messy and perfection is a myth, so know that it is okay if your first attempts at emotional expression do not go particularly well. The point is to *act*, not *prepare*. I would love to provide a true how-to manual for grief, but it doesn't exist because grief doesn't cooperate with a step-by-step approach.

No matter how much you read, no matter the cozy preparations you put in place, no matter the perfect pen or journal, grief emotions will do what they do.

Mental and emotional energy are limited in grief, so do yourself a favor and use the energy you have to go through the process rather than prepare for it. It might be painful. It will likely be exhausting. It will also prevent you from getting stuck, and if there is one guarantee I can give you about grief, it is that continued movement is always better than getting stuck. Use the books, movies, podcasts, and other resources to inform your grief work, not delay it.

Action Challenge

This challenge is especially for the emotional avoiders but will benefit everyone. If there is an area of your grief you know you are avoiding, set an alarm or calendar alert for a daily five- or ten-minute session of intentional grieving. Commit to spend those minutes with nothing more than yourself, a picture or other reminder of the person who died, and possibly a journal. Just sit with the picture or other reminder and allow whatever thoughts and emotions that present themselves to wash over and through you. When the timer sounds, you can choose to turn away from the grief for the rest of the day or continue to sit with it a while longer. Do what is right for you. Just do.

TOOLKIT: EMOTIONAL BRUSHING

This guide is bound to stir up some emotions, and while the processing and expression encouraged through the Toolkits and Reflections are useful, they are sometimes not enough for complete emotional release. Sometimes the waves of grief strike with such impact that standard emotional release practices are not sufficient to fully free you from the force of their weight. Some describe it as a lingering heaviness or a piece of emotion they can't quite access to release. When you have a day with a particularly challenging grief wave or when grief work stirs up more than you were expecting, Emotional Brushing is a tool you can use to rid yourself of troubling remnants. This process, outlined next, may appear too simplistic to be effective, but I urge you to try it. I think you'll be pleased with the results.

Step 1: Plant your feet on the floor to come into full awareness of the moment.

Step 2: Close your eyes and envision where in your body the emotional remnants are disturbing you.

Step 3: Open your eyes and imagine what the remnants look like in your body.

Step 4: Begin brushing away the remnants, just like you would brush away something bothering you, such as when a mosquito buzzes your ear. Starting at your head, run your hands over yourself and down, brushing away from your body with intention. Brush from your head, your shoulders, each arm, your thighs, your calves, and the tops of your feet. Add in any other areas where you feel the remnants linger.

Step 4.5: If you are willing, say goodbye, aloud or in your mind, to what you are brushing from your body. It is not necessary to have an exact name for what you're removing; even "I'm getting rid of the ick!" is enough.

Step 5: Envision everything you just brushed off as a pile on the floor. Sweep it up and dump it in the trash. Ideally, you will literally go through the motions of sweeping, walking to the trash, and throwing the discarded remnants in, but if that is too uncomfortable, simply plant your feet on the floor and imagine the whole process.

Reflection

> "But we do not want you to be uninformed, brothers and sisters, about those who have died, so that you may not grieve as others do who have no hope."
>
> 1 Thessalonians 4:13, NRSV

On the grounds of my alma mater, Hope College in Holland, Michigan, there stands an iconic, massive statue of an anchor. It is the site of countless senior pictures, first-day pictures, graduation pictures, and even engagement pictures; beyond being a perfect photo prop, though, one of the things the statue represents is an image of biblical hope as expressed in Hebrews 6:19. In part, that verse reads, "We have this hope, a sure and steadfast anchor of the soul."

Paul was a wordy, heady guy who did not often speak about emotions in his letters, but this verse from his letter to the Thessalonians captures a departure from that pattern and attunes us to the importance of hope. In those few words, he gives readers both then and today a brief glimpse into an important characteristic of God: God desires us to engage grief and to do so from a place of hope.

Let's not breeze past that first piece. God *wants* you to do your grief work. Grief is a human, natural reaction to death, and as our designer, God is fully aware that we are healthiest when we give ourselves space to process our emotions, and to do so with hope. Hope for more, hope for peace and healing, hope for heaven, hope for continued connection to your person, whatever your source of hope, allow it to sustain you as you grieve.

There is more about hope in the pages ahead, so for today, allow yourself to reflect on how hope already informs your life in general and your grief in particular. Name your hope, not to skip over your grief but to sustain you through the largest storms.

Action Challenge

Take a few moments to consider where in your life you have felt hope and how that hope served you. Look for commonalities among those different scenarios and develop your own definition of hope. Write it here and either mark this page or paste a quote of what you've written in a variety of locations in your home so that you have a concrete reminder of what your hope *is* as you navigate the waves of grief.

To me, hope is . . .

TOOLKIT: ESTABLISH YOUR BELIEFS

A primary purpose of this navigation aid is to help you integrate into your grief process an understanding of how God views grief and how God's view then helps guide how you engage grief. Notice the word "integrate." It is not enough to merely acknowledge that God gives us permission to grieve; that is a surface-level perspective that resides in the mind and does not always lead to action. However, integrating the belief that you may grieve *genuinely* allows you to proceed with grief work that is real and raw, no holds barred, even when it is directed to God.

Proceed through the following steps even if you feel your beliefs about grief are already sufficiently established. Consider your answers a mission statement for your grief work.

Read Genesis 50:1–14 and then consider this quote: "For believers who are also grievers, Joseph is proof positive that having faith in God does not eliminate grief" (*Faith Doesn't Erase Grief*, 81). Write your initial responses or thoughts to both the scripture passage and the quote in this space:

Now, complete the following sentence starters:

The way my faith informs my grief is . . .

About grief, God feels . . .

As a griever who is a believer . . .

Finally, take all the information you compiled and combine it into a statement that outlines your commitment to yourself to continue working through your grief. Incorporate reminders of God's support and encouragement as you feel led. Bonus: If you are willing, contact me with your final statement at katejmeyer.com.

Reflection

> "Unfortunately, the numbness does not last because we are not meant to live free of feelings.... Clients report feeling like they are "going backwards" in their grief.... First and foremost, hear that you are not losing the progress you made. It is in feeling unpleasant emotions that we move forward."
>
> *Faith Doesn't Erase Grief*, 98

Where would we be without Novocain? Stick with me on this. Can you imagine getting a cavity filled—or worse, a root canal—without it? My dentist wrote "TLC" on my chart because I always need more, both in quantity and time for it to be effective, than the average person, and neither of us enjoys it when she starts a procedure before everything has kicked in. Sure, extra Novocain means an extra hour or two of difficult eating and drinking, along with that strange numb sensation in the face from jaw to eye, but every single time, it's been worth it.

And then, somewhere around four to six hours after the procedure, the pain comes. Sometimes it is a gradual sensation, and sometimes it hits unpredictably and with surprising force. Rude, right? Friends, that is the numbness fade. When the Novocain dissipates, the pain you feel isn't new pain. It was there the whole time but masked. The end of the Novocain removed the mask and revealed the pain. In fact, by that point, you are very likely feeling *less* pain—difficult as that is to believe—than you would have otherwise had without the numbness.

God implanted in us a natural numbness to carry us through the early weeks of grief. It allows us to function and complete those initial necessary tasks. That numbness permits grievers to experience the reality of the death in small, endurable doses. Unfortunately, it cannot last forever. The numbness must fade because we cannot live a full life without fully experiencing emotions.

The numbness fade is not a regression in grief; it is not an indicator that you somehow went backward in your progress. Instead, it is a natural step in the process and a signal that your brain is beginning to feel safe again, ready for the next round of experiencing this new reality. It seems counterintuitive, but to feel the whole weight of your grief is another step forward, another step toward returning to active living in the present and dreaming about the future.

Action Challenge

Many people use numbing distractions throughout their initial grief experiences, some healthy and others decidedly not healthy. Distraction is okay and often needed, but avoidance is not. Avoidance is risky because it can lead to becoming entrenched in grief. Consider your coping tools—whether it's reading, calling a friend, watching a favorite movie, going for a walk, sleeping, or hydrating—and evaluate each one's role. Do they temporarily distract you from your grief, or do they encourage avoidance? If most of your coping tools lend themselves to avoidance, consider switching out those tools for healthier ones. If you are unsure if some tools might need to change, remember the Novocain analogy. Novocain allows a short-term endurance of a necessary, unpleasant event, but if that numbness lasted forever, we would find it intrusive and disruptive. If your tools do not include an eventual return to the present uncomfortable reality, they will not provide a long-term benefit. If you need to, write a commitment to yourself to make changes and share it with someone who can lovingly hold you accountable.

TOOLKIT: TAKE A CUE FROM HANNAH

Read Hannah's story in 1 Samuel 1:1–18 before progressing with the remainder of today's exercise. If you are already familiar with Hannah's story, I encourage you to try reading it in a translation that is not your norm. Though the grief on display in this story is not overtly identified as related to human death, I believe we need to maintain the possibility that Hannah did deal with death(s) the author of the biblical text either was not aware of or did not feel necessary to include. But regardless of the cause, Hannah's grief is undeniably real and has something to teach all grievers.

After reading the passage through at least once, proceed through the following prompts and questions:

Go back through the passage and write down every emotion Hannah experiences, including any you feel are present but unnamed.

Describe what you see in your mind's eye when picturing how Hannah appears drunk while praying.

What is your initial reaction to the description you just wrote? Is there a piece of you that desires to feel free enough to emote with the same intensity?

Read verses seventeen and eighteen again. What occurs in verse seventeen, and how is that connected to what is described in verse eighteen?

How did this passage help you understand or reaffirm your understanding of the importance of expressing and releasing emotions?

Capture any additional thoughts on what you learned from Hannah and how you will apply it to your grief going forward.

Reflection

"And then it happens. It comes when you least expect it and without any way for you to stop it: the dam breaks."

Faith Doesn't Erase Grief, 3

Sometimes emotions are gentle. They trickle in based on the experience of the moment and come precisely as expected. Wouldn't it be nice if emotions always functioned that way? Unfortunately, emotions can also show up unannounced at unwelcome times and with a force like water bursting through a dam. On the other side of the barrier, unbeknownst to our everyday awareness, the water built and pressure rose. As the force of water gained strength, the barrier bent and bulged before the water demolished it, flooding anything and everything in its path. Grief emotions often function like that. No barrier we create can withstand the force and power of the waters of grief; we have no choice but to experience them.

There is no practice sufficient to prevent dam-breaking grief. It can arrive without warning and rush over and through us at an intensity that will not be ignored. We immediately lose our footing, and it takes our total focus not to give in to our rising panic. When grief is new, this onslaught of emotion seizes us when our brain is already not functioning at its best, and that makes the entire experience that much more disorienting.

These types of grief waves happen. It is a fact we must accept because denying them does not stop the emotions from bursting through the dam. Accept these waves and face them without fear of experiencing the emotion. How? First, *feel* the emotions. Allow them to wash over you without hindering your expression; keep yourself and others safe, but beyond that, release them.

When a dam breaks, the water goes wherever it wants. The mistake we make when an emotional dam breaks is to try to ignore or discredit our rampant emotions. Trying to stop or manipulate them only leaves more destruction. Instead, let the dam break, and give your full attention to what you think and feel as the grief overruns your inner world. Then, as it dissipates, notice that you are safe. Raw and possibly still in pain, yet safe. Hold fast to this fact. Then, when the next wave comes, you'll be able to face it knowing you'll be okay on the other side.

Action Challenge

To take command of grief waves is primarily about believing you have the power to control what feels completely outside of your control. If you're unfamiliar with emotions or never learned how to effectively express and release them, grief waves can be frightening. Whether you're an emotional novice or an expert, commit to investigating your emotions for the next few days. When an emotion has a name, you can learn about it, and as you learn about it, you will come to recognize that it only has power if it remains unknown. Once it is known, you can face it head-on. Work on naming your emotions, and once you've done so, pair each one with a way to express it so that the next time you feel that emotion, you will remain calm because you know how to handle it.

TOOLKIT: EMOTIONAL EXPRESSIONS

This is one of those pages to bookmark in some way for easy reference. Fill it in as you learn more about your emotions, and keep it easily accessible. Then when you experience a mix of emotions and in the moment can't recall how you last successfully coped with them, return to this table to remind and guide you. If you're in the early months of grief, maybe take a picture of the completed table with your phone for on-the-go access.

A few common examples are pre-filled; add in whatever you already know works for you, and then add to the table as you learn more.

Emotion	Expression	Emotion	Expression
Overwhelmed	Sort tasks on paper	Angry	Hit a pillow, punching bag, etc.
Sad	Allow tears	Lonely	Call a friend & name this truth

Reflection

> "Rather than facing it in the moment, he tried to outrun it. Suffice it to say that did not end well."
>
> *Faith Doesn't Erase Grief*, 58

When asked about the content of the book of Jonah, most people only know the broad strokes of the whole belly-of-the-whale situation. I get it; that's a difficult vignette to beat. It is, though, just one piece of a larger, continuous story that comprises the book of Jonah, a story where we listen in as a prophet works through his relationship with God, and God extends forgiveness and mercy. Perhaps the least-known aspect of Jonah's life are the incidents tucked throughout the book that teach a thing or two about grief.

God gave Jonah a message he did not like, and in that moment, Jonah had a decision to make. Option one was to tell God how he felt about this task and engage God in conversation about his hesitations. Option two was to stuff his reaction, turn, and run.

Jonah opted to run hard and fast in the opposite direction, anything to avoid confronting—let alone expressing before God—the uncomfortable emotions contained in his body. Anything to avoid the inevitable conversation and possible consequence that would follow.

The first message for grievers hidden within the book of Jonah is this: Emotions cannot be outrun. When the fear of experiencing emotion escalates enough, we convince ourselves that we just need to bury what we're feeling, turn our back on it, and it will go away. Then, each time that emotion creeps back in, we throw a little more denial at it to tamp it down. Without fail, though, eventually the emotion garners enough strength that no amount of denial will keep it from breaking through the walls we have built. It will outright demand the expression initially required.

Depending on how long you try to outrun an emotion,

its demand for expression will build in a variety of ways that might include new body aches, changes in eating or sleeping habits, numbing behaviors, or decreased tolerance of others. Subsequently, it's no surprise that the unifying experience for every "Jonah" I meet is exhaustion. No matter how big your emotion or what it will require to express and release it, I promise you it will consume more of your mental, emotional, and physical energy to avoid it. Will facing your looming emotions be difficult? Probably. Painful? Likely. Easy? Unlikely. Worth it? Absolutely.

Action Challenge

If you've been avoiding a particular emotion and worry that facing it will be too much for you to handle, contact a licensed professional who specializes in grief. They will be able to assist you not just with emotional expression but also with processing and releasing, which are often the most avoided parts of emotional engagement.

TOOLKIT: LIKE JONAH, LET IT *ALL* OUT

Jonah is a prophet unafraid to tell God exactly what he feels. Yes, he's delayed at first, but eventually the full spectrum of his emotions comes flying out. In Jonah 2 we see him releasing his emotions through a formal prayer that is reflective of what one would expect from a prophet. In Jonah 4 he presents a different side of himself, showing us what it means to fully empty out your emotional backlog.

The formal prayer in chapter two is centered on gratitude and forgiveness, whereas the temper tantrum (my classifier, not the Bible's) gives Jonah an outlet for all the underlying emotions that led to needing forgiveness in the first place. He's a shining example of how emotional release cannot be halfway because eventually the remainder will demand expression.

Following are only two words. Read them, sit with them for just a few moments, then start writing what you feel or draw what you see. Write without hesitation or intention—just let your subconscious/Spirit take over and dig deep for you. No editing. Just write.

Temper Tantrum

Reflection

"Emotions are natural gifts from God and are valid simply because you feel them."
Faith Doesn't Erase Grief, 56–57.

"I should probably move past this at some point, but . . . ." That was my self-talk the day before writing this Reflection. I am a master at invalidating my own emotions. This behavior, of course, is nothing to be proud of, but I want to be transparent with you so you understand that I live what I write.

I spoke those words after allowing a momentary release of anger that had been triggered as I was venting about a certain situation to a friend. Now, this friend knew the situation and had validated the source of my anger many times over by this point, but as I expressed it in that moment, I became hyperaware that I was in an anger loop—repeating the same story—and felt like I was wasting this friend's time. This is a sneaky form of invalidation. My heart (anger) and brain (fear of inconveniencing my friend) were at war, and the moment I spoke the word "should," my brain won. That also means my heart lost.

You see, I entered that conversation unaware of my risk for an emotional trigger, which meant my defenses were down and the emotion I had been fighting to keep at bay (anger) was free to surface. Unfortunately, as you well know, some emotions carry with them uncomfortable sensations that tend to make us want to shut them down as quickly as possible, and that is exactly what I did. The jitters started, my heart rate accelerated, and I realized I did *not* want to go there. I was tired of going there. I wanted to be *done* going there. I did not believe I was *right* to go there.

Emotions are layered and nuanced and exhausting and complex. They are also natural gifts from God to help us understand our experiences. They are inherent signals that we are experiencing something that needs attention, and because of that, we do not need to waste time or energy determining their legitimacy. Your emotion, whatever it is, is valid simply because it exists.

In grief, emotions routinely surface that appear illogical, pointless, or just plain wrong, yet if an emotion is surfacing, it means the *root* of it needs to be exposed and examined, then either transplanted or removed. The grieving process even means confronting the possibility that after someone's death, you have been left with unresolved conflict. They didn't suddenly turn into a perfect person just because they died. The less-than-ideal parts of your story with them were not erased, and your feelings over this reality are just as valid as any others and deserve to be resolved with respect and compassion.

The next time you catch yourself talking your own self out of feeling something, stop. Instead, examine what you feel with an open heart, and give yourself the grace to experience it.

Action Challenge

Name an emotion you are experiencing but do not believe you should. Explore the source of it and write a letter about it to the person you're mourning. Do you need to finally tell them your true feelings about a situation? Do you need them to forgive you for something? Whatever is tied to this emotion, say it. To your person, to God, to yourself, maybe all three—just get it out of you.

TOOLKIT: UNBURDENING

Grief is heavy and uncomfortable. A lot of it is also uncontrollable. Rather than focusing on what is outside our own control, though, we can choose to take control of and release the burdens that are ours to release. There are emotions or memories you carry that you wish you didn't, and that is okay. It does not mean you love or respect or appreciate the person or your shared experiences any less if you choose not to carry certain things any further in your life. It can in fact be beneficial to release certain feelings and experiences about your person.

To get started with this exercise, list a word or symbol in each boulder on the following page that represents a specific memory, emotion, etc., that you are ready to release. This is just for you, so the word or symbol need only make sense to you. Then, either after each one or once you've filled the page, say goodbye to each boulder. Before you do, take a moment to center yourself: Feel your feet on the ground, inhale a deep breath, then slowly release it. Meditate on each boulder, expressing any related gratitude or acknowledgment of how it influenced your life, and say goodbye.

If you prefer a more in vivo experience, write on actual rocks, then take them with you on a walk. Reflect on them one by one before releasing each to the ground. Whichever way you engage this activity, pay attention to the change in emotional weight you experience. Conclude your time with a brief reflection on any observations or noted changes in the indicated space.

Observations:

Reflection

"Feeling relief or acknowledging things you do not miss does not mean you didn't truly and completely love the person. You are being honest about the full range of your grief emotions."

Faith Doesn't Erase Grief, 100

The summer of 2000 was my second summer working at a Christian camp in Illinois, and it began with a new boss. She hired me based on the recommendations of former staff and placed me in one of the lead positions. I was thrilled! Until the day I messed up.

As is typical of the average nineteen-year-old, I believed I had the routine down and did not need to bother with daily task lists. One particular day, I proceeded with my usual rounds, believing all was well, until my boss called me to her office over the walkie-talkie attached to my hip. I don't care how old you are, getting called to the principal's office will produce a flood of emotions every time. As it turned out, that morning I had missed a significant task that then caused a chain reaction of messes. While I walked around feeling content, enjoying my day, she had cleaned it all up. We talked about a lot of things that morning, including her humbling frustration with me, but what I can still hear clear as day is this: "Jesus said I have to love you—he never said I always have to like you."

Twenty-five years later, those words still pack a punch, yet I have also come to appreciate them because they reflect a truth inherent to all human relationships. No matter how deeply you love a person, there will be times when you are annoyed, angry, and frustrated—in short, times when you do not like them all that much. And that is okay. You are an imperfect person who loves an imperfect person.

This is natural, and it means that you need to grieve the *whole* person. Grieving the things you didn't like—the aspects of their personality you don't miss, even the moments that caused you pain or harm—in no way dishonors the person or the relationship. It is simply honest, and living honestly is how we move forward. And, as a bonus, sometimes remembering those things during a particularly painful grief wave brings a bit of respite, and maybe even laughter.

Action Challenge

To fully honor the person who died means acknowledging—and releasing—those pieces of them that were less than desirable. I have pieces made them them, and you loved them, so grieve their whole being. Take a few moments before leaving this page to bring back to mind those aspects of the person that annoyed you, angered you, frustrated you, left you feeling unseen or unheard. Write them below or talk intentionally with a trusted friend, expressing those things openly. You cannot move forward in grief if you do not grieve the whole person; if you feel stuck, this might get you moving again.

TOOLKIT: GUIDED FREE ASSOCIATION

In my work with clients, I developed an exercise called Guided Free Association to help them uncover those things that need to come to the surface in order for the client to move through and beyond them. In this section, the focus of the exercise is *emotions*. What emotions do you sense you need to explore yet actively avoid because you don't want to face them or fear they will be too much to handle? Are you concerned that you are *not* experiencing a certain emotion? This tool will assist you in answering these and similar questions and help you break free from them. Read through the following steps *before* beginning so you have what you need to move seamlessly through the process.

Step 1: Choose a Focus Word related to your blocked emotions and write it here (i.e., anger, regret, hope).

Step 2: Start a timer for fifteen to thirty seconds and stare at your Focus Word, repeating it in your mind until the timer sounds.

Step 3: Start a timer for ten to fifteen minutes and begin writing on the following blank page. Let your brain take over and allow your words to meander wherever they want to go. Have another sheet of paper or a laptop nearby in case you need more room.

Step 4: When the timer sounds, stop writing. Move from the space where you completed this activity and do something soothing and preferably physical. Take a shower, go for a walk, call a friend. If you want to process what you wrote, I encourage you to do so with a therapist or someone you trust.

Reflection

"God gave us emotions to aid in experiencing life and communicating with God. And if we believe that to be true, then we cannot support the idea that emotions are to be feared or suppressed for any reason."
Faith Doesn't Erase Grief, 50

"I'm afraid if I let myself start crying, I'll never be able to stop." The mother who sat across from me had recently endured the death of one of her children and spoke these very understandable words with a mix of fear and longing. The fear encompassed both what she named—a genuine fear that she would never stop crying—and the impact that embracing those tears would have on her ability to care for her other children, go to work, and take care of herself. The longing was born out of a need to feel differently within her own body.

In other words, her body knew what her mind and heart did not yet feel prepared to accept. Many clients describe it as a buzzing or restlessness. I once had a care provider use the word "fussy." Suppressed emotions can stay in that state, but only for a time. The longer a person waits to express them, the more active these emotions become as they seek an escape from the trap in which they've been placed. That buzzing or restlessness or fussiness that you feel is your emotions hatching their escape plan, and it serves as both a warning bell and a reminder. The warning bell—signaling the inevitable explosion if your emotions are not soon released—is likely the more familiar of the two to you, but the reminder is a gift. That sensation in your body is your reminder that no matter how big or intimidating, emotions need to be expressed because in expression we find *relief*. Sometimes, we even find freedom.

I understood this woman's fear and her longing, and it was only when she said those words that I realized she had yet to cry in any of our sessions together. Over the next few sessions, we worked together to find modes of expression that felt safer, and she steadily increased her practice of those tools. At first, she practiced them only with me, but then she advanced to practicing in moments and areas she considered safe at home. Eventually she allowed her spouse and children to witness her grief. The first session after she permitted them to see her pain, she arrived with a new lightness. The pain was still evident in her eyes and demeanor—how could it not be—yet I could see her body was relaxed for the first time since her child's death.

From this relaxed posture she discovered a regained ability to *connect* with her family and learned that if they all were honest and shared their grief with each other, the load was a bit easier to bear.

Action Challenge

Create a "baby steps" plan for giving release to the big emotions you are suppressing. You are *not* required to experience the full brunt of them in one sitting. Incremental steps will get you to where you need to be in a safe, gracious manner. Plus, each time you take a step, you prove to yourself that you *can* bear some of the experience of the emotion, and that is a priceless affirmation. To get you started, consider the following possible incremental steps: sitting with the person's picture and allowing emotions to flow freely for five minutes; using their name in conversations; experimenting with release practices like crying, running, or popping bubble wrap; or doing one activity you've avoided and asking a trusted person to join you.

Reflection

"The most damaging misconception about emotions is that they are either positive or negative."
Faith Doesn't Erase Grief, 51

"Don't sin by letting anger control you."
Ephesians 4:26, NLT

Before reading further, take a moment to reread that first quote and circle which of the following is true for you: (1) I disagree, emotions *are* positive or negative; (2) I agree, emotions are neutral.

Most of us probably would circle number one, but the reality is that emotions, in and of themselves, are neither positive nor negative. Now, the neutrality of emotions might seem like an insignificant factor of everything you're currently facing, but what we believe about emotions directly correlates with either forward movement or getting stuck in grief. The reason for that is simple: When we believe an emotion is bad, we are more likely to ignore, deny, or suppress it until it explodes out of us, and that keeps a griever stuck. Emotions are simple signposts or status signals that God built into us to guide us through our experiences, nothing more and nothing less. The positive and negative elements we associate with emotions arise in how we choose to express them.

Scripture has a lot to say and show about emotions, but I chose this verse from Ephesians because anger is perhaps the emotion most often listed in the bad column. It is also an emotion often found in grief. First, notice the verse embraces the existence of anger. Anger is a real emotion, equally bestowed by God upon humanity as any other emotion, and it can signal injustice, betrayal, defeat, regret, and much more; because of that, the last thing we should do is ignore it. Second, this verse reminds grievers that we can *choose* to what degree anger controls our thoughts, words, and actions.

The logical question, then, is how do we prevent anger—or any emotion—from taking control and consuming our hearts, bodies, and minds? The answer is to find a healthy way to express it. Expression of an emotion validates it the moment you speak it, which allows you to begin facing and releasing it, and this depletes its control over you.

When an emotion is classified as positive, it is tempting to hide yourself within it and ignore any emotions classified as negative—but the walls constructed to maintain long-term avoidance of "negative" emotions eventually remove the ability to feel *anything*. When emotions are viewed as neutral, however, the griever can embrace all of them equally, moving through them without shame, fear, or hesitancy.

Action Challenge

If you feel stuck in your grief, there is likely a component of unexpressed emotion. Through journal writing or conversation with a therapist, explore what emotions you are avoiding or denying and why. Once these are identified, begin the process of reframing the emotion from "bad" to "neutral," and then list some healthy ways you might express that emotion. Try each healthy expression you come up with, note the ones that are successful for you, and then file your list away for easy access the next time a similar emotion surfaces.

TOOLKIT: WHERE DOES IT HURT?

Anxiety's physiological manifestation is so well-known that we have an expression for it embedded in the common vernacular: "butterflies in the stomach." And what about "ants in the pants" or "elephant on the chest"? These too communicate the bodily presence of emotion. The fact of the matter is that emotions typically include a bodily response that increases the longer we ignore them.

Now, I will admit, this exercise is one I most often see applied in children's grief groups, but frankly, adults also benefit from learning the cues their emotions send through their bodies. These cues are your body's way of saying, "Hey! Attention! You need to stop ignoring this before something bad happens."

To that end, draw an outline of your body on the next page. Make it sizable enough that you can differentiate the head, chest, and stomach; arms and hands; and legs and feet, and each section should be large enough to accommodate one or more emotions. Then find some markers or crayons and assign a color to each emotion you already know has a sensation in your body. Color each one in the appropriate place.

Earmark this page and add to the drawing whenever you discover something new; use it to help you understand what you might be feeling, especially if there is no physical cause for the symptom. Note: When in doubt, please check with your doctor.

Reflection

"Emotions are varied and nuanced. The basic emotions are but umbrella terms for the more nuanced emotions found within a certain category."

Faith Doesn't Erase Grief, 50

Every pigment humanity has managed to create is a blend of at least two primary colors, right? Every color goes back to red, yellow, or blue. Think of emotions in a similar fashion. Unlike color, there is not a uniform understanding of the number of basic emotions, but for simplicity's sake, we'll assume there are four: happiness, sadness, anger, and fear. As you look at the Emotions List at the front of this section, you will notice that some specific emotions flow from one basic emotion and others flow from a combination of at least two basic emotions.

Consider, for instance, the word "grateful." At first glance, this would appear to be a feeling that flows only from the basic emotion of happiness. There are situations, however, when it might equally flow from the basic emotion of anger. In other words, a person who is grateful as they remember a loved one might simultaneously feel a general gratitude (happiness) for the time they had with the person *and* disbelief (anger) that there will not be more.

In grief, the experience of multiple emotional reactions to one situation is common. Fight against the discomfort of that or the need to keep your emotions strictly separated. Remember that grief is a season of both/and, and this applies to emotions as much as anything. Oftentimes you will not feel just one thing. That is normal, and you can adapt to existing in this tension. You can use the Emotions List to help you identify the nuances of what you feel. Though the blending of emotions is not always comfortable, remember that the simultaneous experience of seemingly contradictory emotions can result in a greater depth of awareness that reveals a unique beauty. I think we can agree that we all could use a little beauty in the landscape of grief.

Action Challenge

The Emotions List is not exhaustive. When you are full of a combination of many emotions and nothing on the list satisfactorily captures them, create your own name for the composite. Play with this! It can be surprisingly satisfying to give a name of your own creation to the blob of emotions within. If you come up with something that works for you, add it to the list. You never know when you might need it again.

TOOLKIT: GRACE

Perfection is never attainable, and that is never truer than during grief. If you already completed the Toolkit on healthy emotional expression (see page 39), you know that we prepare such lists because there is such a thing as *unhealthy* emotional expression. The fact of the matter is that the parts of you that you like the least will likely show themselves sometime during the Early and Middle phases of grief. Because grief amplifies emotions, it is best to view these moments as inevitable and prepare now for what you will do in and after those moments to show yourself grace.

Step 1: Forgiveness

Seek forgiveness from someone for the impact of your emotional explosion and/or extend it to yourself.

Step 2: Planning

Evaluate what occurred prior to and during the explosion. What elements were within your control, and which were not? What warning signs can alert you that it is time to healthily express an emotion *before* it reaches the level of explosion? How can you set yourself up for an improved chance not to repeat the most recent experience? Jot down notes here and return as needed to add or remove suggestions for yourself.

Step 3: Grace

This third step will be easy to skip, but I challenge you to complete it. You need to be kind and gentle with yourself more than ever while grieving; in other words, extend yourself grace. If you need an example, try the following: On a slow, steady inhale, say in your mind, "I am human." While holding that breath, say in your mind, "Mistakes are natural." On a forceful, long exhale, say in your mind, "And I am not defined by them." If that does not work for you, that's okay! Find your own way(s) to extend yourself grace. That is what matters here.

Reflection

> "Grief imbued with hope is felt the first time you laugh after your person's death."
>
> *Faith Doesn't Erase Grief*, 25

Hope is a state of being that cannot be defined, at least not satisfactorily, but when you feel it, you know it. Grief is a season of life in which hope can be difficult to find, let alone feel, and yet hope is the cushion that sustains grievers through the choppiest grief waves. How does that work?

Let's use laughter as an example. Laughter in grief is hard to come by, especially for natural criers, and for many of us, it is difficult to imagine ever laughing again. It might start reappearing slowly, disingenuous and obligatory in a social setting, because this is easier than drawing the negative attention that would follow our *not* laughing. Next is the light chuckle in conversation with a safe person, and then, out of nowhere, the first true, genuine laugh breaks free. It might catch you off guard, or maybe you inadvertently contrived it by watching something that consistently results in a laugh. The *how* doesn't matter; what matters is that it happened. You thought it would never happen again, and then it did.

This is how hope functions too. It does not eliminate the pain. It does not change reality. It *does* give a little boost, a momentary respite, and the breath you are able to take during that respite is everything. Embrace the experience of grief and seek hope (and laughter) along the way. They will surely sustain you through every wave of grief.

Action Challenge

Choose a way to store up your hope. In other words, when the hope is palpable, capture the details surrounding when you felt it and store them in some way that allows you to return to that feeling when needed.

TOOLKIT: WORDLESS EMOTIONS JOURNALING

I typically call this "emotions journaling" but added "wordless" to the title to not scare away those of you who fear traditional journaling. Hey, I get it—"journaling is not for everyone" (though, secretly, I think it is)! So here's my compromise. This tool is simple, can be as fast as you want it to be, and is perfect for when you feel full of emotions but cannot find the words to express them. All you need to complete this process are some colored pencils, markers, paints, or crayons, a journal or two pieces of paper, and the Emotions List found at the start of this section (page 15–16).

Once you have your materials, read through the Emotions List, paying attention to any that stir something within you. For each emotion word that does, assign a color to it and indicate that on one piece of paper. If you're using a bound journal, dedicate a page to be the color key to reference during repeat use of this tool. Once you have a color assigned to each emotion that resonates with you, start adding color to the next page in ways that represent the bundle of emotions you're feeling inside. Maybe one color is only a small blob, and two other colors consume the remainder of the space. Maybe some have sharp edges, or some are very light while others are heavy. Turn off your conscious brain and let the colors flow, and pay attention to how your body feels as you pour the emotions onto the page.

TOOLKIT: TRAJECTORY TRACKER 1

This tool reflects the fact that grief is not steady, linear, predictable, or unidirectional. Here the adage of "one step forward, two steps back" does not apply, though it might feel like it does. The Trajectory Tracker is here to help you in this confusing reality to visualize where you are and where you want to be. Be sure to date a trajectory when you complete it so you can later compare it to others. Hopefully in this way, over time, you will clearly see that you have moved forward overall. If you compare the completed trackers and find that you have *not* moved forward, consider that an indicator you should reach out for more help.

On the next page you will see an image of a path with three main areas: Start, Middle, and Beyond. *Start* indicates the place or time when your thoughts and actions are stuck in the past, with minimal participation in the present and no thoughts of the future. *Middle* signals a shift to a state where you are living more in the present, able both to remember the past without getting caught up in it and to envision the future. *Beyond* is the final stage of the path where you now fully participate in daily life and actively work on building toward the future. You have learned how to carry your person's presence with you as you desire and to control when to reflect and remember.

Considering those three main areas, reflect on where you are in the present moment. Are you close to the start, firmly in the middle, or somewhere between? Place a mark along the pathway, indicating the date, to show where you think you are at this point, and add a few comments or sentences about why you placed yourself there. Then write a goal for where you want to be when you complete the next tracker.

Date:

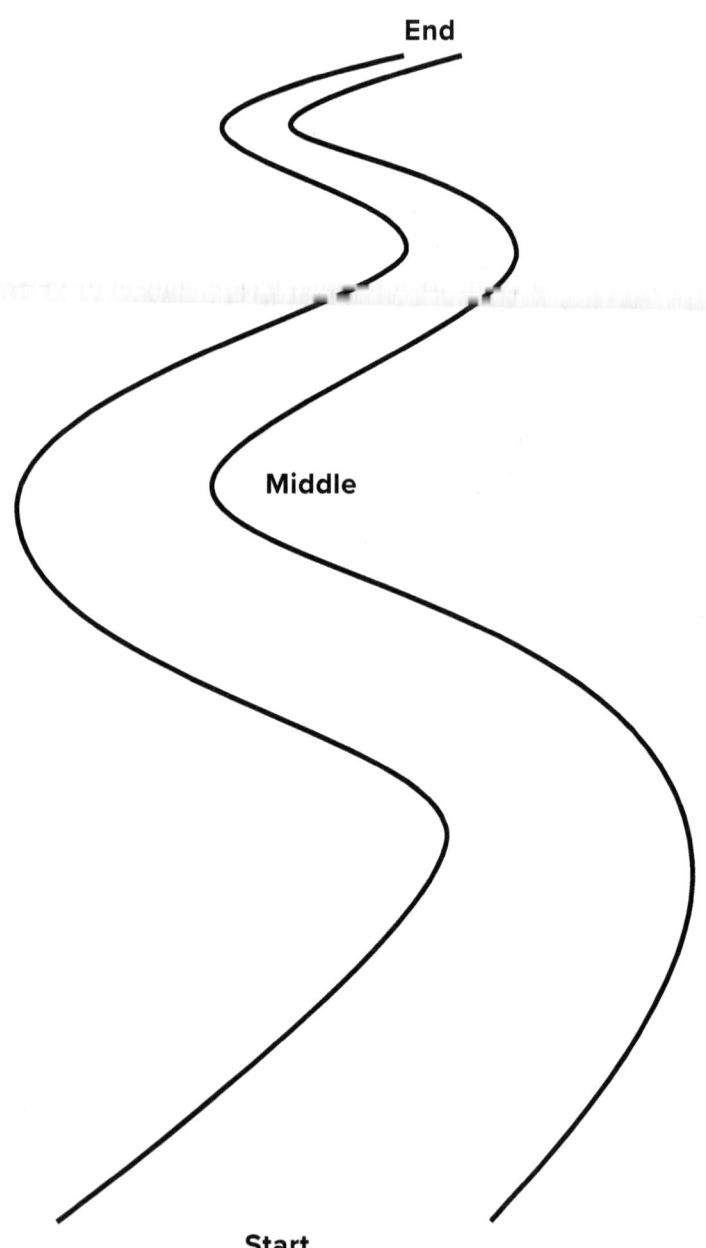

Connection

We are beings created to exist in connection with God, self, and others, yet in Early Grief, people often feel cut off in every sense: isolated and alone, unaware even of themselves, walking through their days numb and barely aware. This isolation is only one of the lies perpetuated by grief, but it is a common culprit for trapping grievers in the worst segments of the journey.

In this section, all Toolkit and Reflection pages address at least one aspect of connection—with God, self, or others—and some address all three. The general focus of each entry is on helping you return to awareness of God's presence, to a sense of reconnection with yourself, and to a desire to again connect with others in ways both related and unrelated to the person who died and your grief. In this portion we will also explore what it means to continue in a changed relationship with the person who died. Take your time with those pages in particular, especially if the idea of a continued relationship is an unfamiliar or uncomfortable topic for you. I want to encourage you to try, though: If you allow yourself to push through that discomfort, your heart will thank you.

A word of notice: This is not about necessarily *liking* all the people you reconnect with, nor is it about accepting the status quo if you find some relationships need adjustment. It is merely about returning to awareness of these relationships, including within yourself, and gaining the ability to recognize what is acceptable as is, what needs to change, and what you need or desire to leave behind as you continue forward.

    The Toolkits and Reflections in this section might require more mental and emotional energy than the other sections, so I recommend saving this section for days when you can truly engage it without distraction or rushing through. Create a safe space and time to go deeper, to explore, and to excavate. As you dwell in that intentional space, be prepared for unexpected gifts. You will know what I mean when you experience one. Write down the gift when it happens and record the date; it's a treasure you're going to want to refer back to in the months and years ahead.

TOOLKIT: OBJECT LESSON

If you had to illustrate your grief, what would it look like? The image that most resonates with me is that of a large internal ball with sharp edges that poke and prod, inflicting pain from head to toe with each movement I take. Then, as I work at it, it slowly shrinks in size, and the spikes fall off. Draw what your grief looks like and how you carry it in your body. Is it all-consuming? Maybe it's on the smaller side, so that it bounces around your body? Are its edges, sharp, dull, or some of each? Is it small enough that you can keep it in one place, tucked away where it causes minimal pain? Draw (or describe with words if that's more of your thing) what is true of you and your grief right now, and record the date.

Reflection

> "But we are not meant to live in grief 24/7/365 for the remainder of life; instead, we need to be able to continue growing and becoming the people we are created to be. There is more to learn, more to do, and more people to love. That doesn't mean your connection to your person disappears; it means that connection changes, evolves into something new that leaves room for your life to continue."
>
> *Faith Doesn't Erase Grief*, 36

Have you ever avoided something that had the promise to help you because of the fear that it wouldn't work? This happens a lot. People stay in unhealthy cycles because the known quality of them produces a greater sense of security than stepping into an unknown—especially when our brains tell us that the unknown has a 50/50 chance of *not* being better than what already exists. Often, however, when we do take that step, it provides needed change, growth, or progress.

For grievers, one manifestation of this fear is the "shutdown," the refusal to reengage in life. After all, life as it was is gone, and the world feels unfamiliar. Even deeper than this lies the fear that reengaging with life will result in losing every last lingering connection you have to the person who died: their voice, their face, their imprint.

The truth is that your relationship with your person has changed, but not ended. Yes, their physical presence is no longer in this world, and that creates a vacant space that feels vast, especially in the early months after their death. But a person is much, much more than their physical presence. A person is ideas, memories, influence, and many other things—none of which are lost in death or when you reengage in life.

As with everything in grief, accepting this idea will not be an immediate transition. You need time to trust that your ongoing connection to your person, changed though it is, is not vulnerable to the Grief Thief, and you gain that trust through openness and practice. To begin, ask yourself if you're even willing to consider a continued connection. Are you hoping this means they will reach out to you in some way—and are you afraid of how you will feel if they don't? Are you simply seeking their continued presence as sustained by friends and family members? Maybe you just want a quiet awareness of repeated signs that remind you of them.

Once you know how you want this to work and what you want out of it, you can practice incorporating it into your daily life. Be intentional about staying open and aware of different ways they might reach out, be it through the repeated presence of an animal or a seemingly random familiar scent or song, and when you encounter those things, record them. Write them down or tell a friend. Consider thanking your person for them. With practice, what might feel strange or even silly at the start will occur without effort. Eventually, you will have a day, for example, when you are out with a friend talking about your latest travel experience, and the truth will hit you: You enjoyed that vacation thoroughly. The physical presence of your person was not with you, but you felt them cheering you on the whole time. Your relationship with them did not end; it changed. And you can still access it.

Action Challenge

Here are some questions to reflect on if you need to establish or find a better connection to your person: What type of connection do you need to feel safe, at peace, and ready to return to your life? Do you need to talk or write to them every day? Are you open to naming that pressure you felt on your shoulder as their presence? Could you acknowledge the little things that make you feel like they are reaching out to you, such as a meaningful item or animal that frequently reappears in your daily life?

If you already have an established connection, consider the

following ways to assure yourself you can have that connection anywhere and anytime: Leave the home. Return to work. Meet new friends. Go back to that place you have avoided since the death. Listen to music or watch movies you both enjoyed. Pay attention to how it feels to take steps back into your life even while you keep your person with you—in whatever way, and for whatever length of time, is right for you.

TOOLKIT: IT'S NOT TOO LATE

It is a common misconception that when a person dies, the chance to find resolution, forgiveness, or reconciliation dies with them. While that is true in the strictest of definitions, the reality is that those experiences are not out of reach if you are willing to get a bit outside of your comfort zone. Each of the following exercises can be applied to resolution, forgiveness (given or received), and reconciliation as well as most anything else left unfinished at the time of death. Try the exercises in any order, though of course I do encourage you to try each, if only to see what best fits your personality. Additionally, if you are working on forgiveness, for example, and find that the first activity does not quite complete the task, try another approach. It is possible your need or concern is deeper than you realize and will require a few different rounds to resolve.

Conversation: This exercise is likely the one most outside of your comfort zone, but try not to let that stop you—it is often the most powerful! Sit facing an empty chair, or place the person's picture or another object of theirs on the chair, and voice aloud all that you need to say. Hold nothing back. Be completely honest, either about your own actions or about their actions and how you were impacted by them, what you long for, what you regret—whatever follows the words "I just wish I had . . ." Keep going until you feel you are done.

To take this further, do that and then add the step of moving to the other chair and verbalizing what they would say to you. It will be tempting to give voice to what you *worry* they would say, but instead, try to channel everything you know about their character and the history of your relationship, and allow that to guide the words that flow.

Letter Writing: Write a letter and pour out everything you wish you could say. Just get it all out onto the page. Simple as it might seem, letter writing will allow you to stop fixating on everything left unaddressed and move forward. To go deeper, write out a conversation between the two of you, using either your nondominant hand or a different color ink for their part of the conversation. Again, channel what you know of their character in their responses, not what you fear they would say. There can be a lot of healing power in seeing their words on paper.

Ritual: This practice can stand alone or be applied as a final step to either Conversation or Letter Writing. It works best, depending on your goal, with either plant seed paper or dissolving paper; you can find these in hobby shops or online. If there is something you need to release or free yourself or the person from, use the dissolving paper. For things that you want a reminder of, such as an expression of reconciliation or an exchange of love, use the seed paper.

Once you choose your paper, write a short message or a phrase that represents what you want to let go of (dissolving paper) or foster (seed paper). Then, when you are ready, center yourself with deep breaths, feel your feet on the ground, and either swirl the dissolving paper in a bowl of water or plant the seed paper in the ground. Close the time of ritual with a promise to yourself that you will remember it any time the burden you just worked through attempts to return, and take a final cleansing breath to signal the end of the ritual.

Reflection

"Of all the things grief steals, the ability to feel love, either from God or towards God, is perhaps the greatest loss."
Faith Doesn't Erase Grief, 20

Author Patrice Karst wrote *The Invisible String* to teach children about grief and continued connections to those we love. The book portrays an invisible string from the heart of the child to their deceased parent: a permanent connection that nothing can sever. Feeling connection with and love for and from the person who died is often the most natural part of the initial grief process. I will address how that connection changes and how it is experienced over time throughout the remainder of this section, but today I want to focus on the fact that our connection to God is, for many, difficult to find in grief. That loss has the power to *un-anchor* you.

A dropped anchor ensures the location of a boat is set, but its position and stability are *not* impacted by the anchor, nor does the anchor promise to protect the boat through a storm. In other words, the waves still come, and they still rock the boat—but at least once the storm has passed, the crew can find their bearings. For grieving believers, the love of God functions like an anchor, so when that connection is interrupted, it causes disorientation and aimless wandering. Waves that crash during those times feel extra worrisome because any confidence that all will be well, come what may, is missing.

Note that connection itself does not guarantee any particular quality of relationship. Believers can still be connected to God even when they do not consider a relationship with God a priority in the moment. In order to hold yourself steady, to reassure yourself that you are ultimately safe no matter the waves that come, reestablishing and maintaining mere connection with God is crucial even when the quality of the relationship is perhaps not ideal. Grievers have described this to me in many ways, but the most impactful image comes from a friend of mine after the death of a parent. During one of our conversations, she shared that "God and I aren't speaking right now." *That* is the sort of basic, fundamental connection I'm referring to. Awareness of God's presence and acknowledgment of continued belief balanced with current questions, anger, doubt, or other feelings—the spiritual version of the silent treatment.

God understands the message in those moments: "I want to call out to you, but I can't. I see you, but I am not ready to engage with you." And you know what? God whispers back to our hearts, "Okay. I'll be here when you're ready to lay it out, and I will walk beside you as you go, just in case." Regardless of what you and God need to sort out, it's worth protecting that connection. Find your anchor point. It won't prevent the waves, but it will provide a sense of security that the waves will not defeat you.

Action Challenge

Take inventory of your connection with God. Is it complete, broken, or severed? Thanks to grief brain, it can be difficult to sort out the nuance here, so draw a line down the middle of the following page and title one column "Connection" and the other "Relationship." When you reflect on God, write what comes to mind in one of the two columns; this should help bring you clarity.

TOOLKIT: LISTENING TO THE SILENCE

Grievers know better than most that sometimes silence is the loudest noise of all. In fact, grievers often leave on the radio or fall asleep to the TV just to avoid the impact of the silence. In other words, we fill that silence because to dwell in it, to fully experience it, forces us to face the reality of who *should* be there. In the silence, their absence is far too present. Yet the reason we avoid silence is the very reason we need to, at least at times, sit in it and truly listen. The following process is a simple one that I encourage you to try multiple times, especially when you feel heavy with emotion or disconnected from yourself, God, or the one you're grieving.

Silent Listening: Find a quiet spot where you can fully attend to the silence around you. Take a piece of paper or a notebook with you, and get in a comfortable position. Close your eyes to remove visual distractions, and just listen within your being. When something occurs to you, write it down so your brain knows it does not need to worry about forgetting it, and then continue listening.

Try to stick with this time of listening for about ten minutes. When the weight of the silence dissipates, either entirely or at least to a more comfortable level, transition slowly out of it. Open your eyes, take a few deep, cleansing breaths, and express gratitude for what you have learned, heard, or released.

Do note, people have been known to fall asleep during this process. Given the way grief fatigues a person, this is not surprising. If you feel yourself drifting off to sleep, do not fight it. That just might be what the silence wanted to tell you.

TOOLKIT: CONNECTION CORNER

"The purpose of the connection corner is to have a guaranteed space for you to go be with and talk to your person whenever and however you desire."

Faith Doesn't Erase Grief, 127

The connection corner can be a room, a literal corner, or a chair; it can be as big and ornate or as small and simplistic as you desire. The point is to set aside a space you know is waiting for you, especially when the people around you stop saying the person's name, stop telling stories about them, and go through significant days as if they aren't even missed. When this happens, you can use the connection corner to check in with the person you are grieving, God, or perhaps both, depending on your need.

Use the following space to gather ideas for your connection corner. Consider all your senses when planning. What textures give you comfort? Will peppermint or cinnamon candy soothe you? Would you like to have your person's favorite treat with you? What scent, music, or other representation of them (a picture, clothing, or familiar item) do you want with you? How about a journal? A Bible? Once your ideas are gathered, plan how you will bring this space to physical fruition. Whether you need it only for a month or for an unforeseen amount of time, your connection corner will serve you well throughout your grief.

Reflection

> "God's love is inescapable, no matter where we need to go with God in our darkest moments. It is normal and expected to consider, explore, and even reevaluate faith during grief."
>
> *Faith Doesn't Erase Grief*, 17

Grief elicits inevitable questions about God. In most spheres of life, we agree that questions are normal and necessary, that from questions comes growth, and therefore questions are encouraged. The one sphere where that has unfortunately not been true is religion. Historically, Christian religious institutions tend to shut down questions with shame, dismissal, or a threat of disconnection from God, community, or both. What, then, is a person to do when they are racked with questions in their grief?

The answer is to go ahead and ask them. Be honest with the range of emotions you feel toward God and/or the church. Rather than ignoring a need to explore or unpack your connection with God or your community, allow yourself the freedom to follow that path where it needs to go. Despite what most believers are taught throughout their lives, God will not leave you while you wander, and God will be there if and when you want to fully reengage. God will not turn away from you for anything you think or say while you sort things out. God created you, knows how the human brain functions in grief, and understands that you do not have the energy to polish your tone or your words.

Even if that means researching other belief systems. Even if that means never again stepping foot in a church. Even if that means skipping Easter. Even if that means being angry with God and questioning the full foundation of your worldview. **Even if you are not sure you still believe.**

Let yourself go there, wherever there is, without fear of repercussion from God. No matter how far you stretch that thread of connection or how bare it becomes, God's loving arms will be open and waiting when you're ready. If you need to yell at God, trust that the love of God, which is broader, deeper, and purer than we can imagine, is big enough not to be shaken while you release all your anger, all your doubt, and all your fear. God's connection to you does not stop—even when you mute your connection to God. It cannot be destroyed.

Action Challenge

What roadblock are you currently facing that is keeping you from fully exploring the faith aspects of your grief? How can you move around that obstruction or destroy it to clear a path forward? Write out your goal and then develop the plan to get from where you are to where you want to be. Even if you want your relationship with God to remain as it is right now, consider what you need to do to ensure that happens.

TOOLKIT: THE INESCAPABLE GOD

Look up Psalm 139 and read it through a few times, particularly verses one through eighteen. If you are already familiar with it, challenge yourself to read it through the lens of a griever. How does it inform your grief to think of God as inescapable? Each time you read the passage, jot down a few reactions to it—as always, freely and without self-judgment.

Reflection

> "Death steals a person, every facet of them."
> *Faith Doesn't Erase Grief*, 7

Secondary losses are aspects of the person that you might not even know you miss until you encounter them again. You might hear something, or see, smell, or taste it, and suddenly you realize how long it's been since you experienced that thing with your loved one. As you adapt to the overall loss of a physical presence, these secondary losses reveal themselves. Sometimes slowly, sometimes in abundance, and often when least expected. You might catch a whiff of cologne, perfume, or lotion while walking in a crowd; maybe a song from the soundtrack of your friendship comes on; or you arrive at someone's home and they serve you a favorite meal your person made or loved; or construction reroutes you, and you suddenly find yourself driving by *that* restaurant, park, store, or other landmark.

We connect with people in a million different ways, which is why the goal of grief work is not to "get better" but to integrate the absence into your continued living. Practically speaking, this means that when you experience a secondary loss, you need to decide what to do with it. Maybe it is enough to sink into the moment of memory, or maybe the reminder created a need to have more exposure to what you've lost. We cannot do anything to restore them physically, but secondary losses often can be restored, at least to some degree.

For instance, consider buying a candle or a bottle of their fragrance so that you can surround yourself with their scent when desired. You might create a computer file filled with pictures of them and any videos that hold their voice, where you can keep them securely tucked away in day-to-day life but accessible when you want them. Maybe this person was your adventure partner, so how might you bring adventure back into your life in a way that meets your need and honors what they fostered in you?

To keep yourself moving forward through grief, allow yourself to reconnect to your person through at least one or even a handful of secondary losses. You might be surprised at how much comfort this provides.

Action Challenge

Choose a secondary loss resulting from the death of your person and allow yourself to reclaim it and reconnect with them. Maybe it is listening to an avoided song, going for a bike ride, or making or buying a favorite meal. Maybe it is something bigger, like returning to a favorite vacation destination. Whatever you choose, do so with intention, and pay attention to how your person shows up through it. Record the experience in some way so that you can revisit it on a day when you need a little extra comfort.

TOOLKIT: GOD JAR

One of the greatest lies of the Grief Thief is that there is no more hope, nothing deserving of gratitude, and no evidence that God remains present. The truth is that these things do remain, though it can be challenging to recognize them for what they are. The God Jar gives you a place to capture any glimmers of hope, sources of smiles, and moments that brought respite from the depths of grief so that when those things are impossible to feel or see, you can look to the jar for concrete evidence that God remains active all around you.

Whether you use the drawing on the next page or a literal jar at home begin recording moments of hope or gratitude and leaving them in the jar. Keep a stack of sticky notes or a scrap paper near the jar at home, and have a note on your phone dedicated to this practice so that you can do it when you're out. In addition, purposefully take time each day to reflect on where you saw or felt God. Did anything surprise you? Did anything make you laugh? Did someone reach out in an unexpected way? Maybe you felt your loved one's presence for the first time since their passing. Whatever goodness you can find, write it down and add it to the jar.

Some days you'll add a lot, and you will also likely have days when you have nothing to contribute, but the more intentional you are about staying alert for any glimmers of goodness and keeping track of them when they happen, the more you train yourself to recognize that you still have access to hope and comfort. What fills the God Jar won't change what you're going through, but seeing the evidence of God's loving presence fill the jar will sustain you.

Reflection

> "When someone dies, expectedly or not, your being longs to continue that conversation."
>
> *Faith Doesn't Erase Grief,* 89

The widower seated across from me wept for his spouse. *Wept.* He arrived each week with a smile that stayed on his face until we cleared the lobby, and then in the safety of my office, he settled into a chair and wept.

And then, one day, a quarter of the way through our session, I noticed that he had yet to shed a tear, let alone weep. I knew him well enough at this point that I believed the change was genuine and not a defense mechanism, yet it also felt abrupt to me. When I pointed it out to him and asked what he thought had shifted, he said, "I finally just started writing to her."

He had tried to connect with his wife in a variety of ways since she died but struggled to find anything consistent and genuine; he had also acknowledged feeling uncertain whether his religion *allowed* him to seek any kind of continued relationship with his wife. But when he realized that he was not making any forward progress, he finally opted for one more attempt.

When his wife was alive, they started each day of their retirement years sitting together at the kitchen table, with their post-breakfast cups of coffee, reading their Bibles and devotionals and writing in their journals. Sometimes they talked about what they read or experienced; other times one finished earlier than the other and went about their day.

On that first day of trying something new, my client went through this normal daily routine alone, but he ended it by writing a letter to his wife. Over time he incorporated reading scripture from her Bible as well as his own. He enjoyed seeing her markings and comments and realized he could still learn new things about her. He wrote to her daily, sometimes twice daily, for about two months before his need to do so slowly faded. Without realizing it, he went back to reading scripture solely for his own spiritual growth, and the letters to his wife grew more infrequent. When he did still write, it happened organically, at unpredicted times.

Because of how his wife's disease had progressed, their rituals and conversations had ended well before she died. It was only after she died, when my client was no longer focused on caring for her, that he realized he needed to finish their conversations. For him that meant writing letter after letter until he felt resolution. The process of concluding conversations or resolving conflict after a person has died is different for everyone, but it *can* be done if you are open to the possibility.

Action Challenge

The way you speak to and with your person is going to be personal to your needs, and it might take a bit of exploration. Trial and error is your friend here. Perhaps you'll feel their presence most in conversation while in nature; perhaps in a letter or at their grave; perhaps by sending an email or texting their number. Maybe you need a combination of approaches. Commit to exploring different options until you find the connection approach that works best for you, and use it until it no longer feels necessary. Then you can trust that it will be there should you ever need it again.

TOOLKIT: HORIZON LINE

"The road of grief is often like hiking in a sand dune. It is long and challenging with no indication of relief. But as you near the water, you feel a breeze, and you come over the final hill to something unexpected and beautiful. The horizon greets you with a promise of continued life, renewed purpose, and *the hope that you will carry your loved one with you into your next adventure.*"

Faith Doesn't Erase Grief, 41, emphasis added

You can find this activity in three different sections of the book, each with a slightly different emphasis depending on the theme of that section. Today I want you to consider what the horizon might look like as it represents a comfortable, desired, continued connection with the person who died. What is in the foreground? What awaits you in the distance? What is the promise beyond the horizon? How close are you to reaching it? If you connect with the sand dune image in the opening quote, consider whether you are still climbing the dune or cresting it with a close view of the water. Do you prefer a desert scene? Or perhaps a cityscape? Reread the opening quote, listen to what stirs in your heart and mind, and draw what you envision around the following horizon line. If drawing intimidates you, that's okay. Use color or words around the line to represent an image that resonates for you.

Reflection

> "The changed relationship is like every other aspect of grief in that it is something available to you as long as you need it."
>
> *Faith Doesn't Erase Grief,* 170

In her third counseling session, the woman told me, with her head hung in shame, that she sleeps in her husband's robe. I let that news sit between us in silence until she raised her eyes back up to mine, at which point I smiled and assured her that she was doing nothing wrong or abnormal. She then told me about the evening ritual she had created to help her transition to bedtime, which was when she allowed herself to express whatever grief-related emotions or thoughts she had pushed aside throughout the day. It was a time when she could talk to her husband without any limitations.

She asked me how long she could continue to do this. I told her what I tell every client when they ask a version of this question: "Don't worry about that now. If it needs to change, it will." She looked at me, as all clients do in response to that statement, with an expression that clearly communicated she did not believe she would naturally arrive at a point of changing, let alone stopping, the ritual.

Throughout the remainder of her time with me, this woman's connection with her husband's robe did in fact change, from wearing it to laying it next to her on the bed to hanging it on the bathroom door, and finally to storing it away. Some steps were separated only by weeks, others by months, but what was consistent was her surprise at each progression. She learned to listen within herself, learned step-by-step that the robe was only a symbol of the permanent connection that would never be severed. Even if the robe was nowhere near her, she learned she could commune with her husband however and whenever she needed. Though his physical presence would never return, she came to trust that on future days when his absence felt glaring, she would be able to connect with him in meaningful ways.

Action Challenge

Before you end today's time of intentional grief work, spend a few moments engaging in your changed relationship with your loved one. What do you want them to know? What about them are you most grateful for today? When were you last caught off guard by the sense of their presence from a sight, sound, taste, or smell? Tell them about the most recent grief work milestone you've reached, such as feeling more happiness than pain when you remember them, laughing out loud, or leaving the house for something enjoyable. Including them in your process helps move you forward.

TOOLKIT: GRIEVING BOTH SIDES OF THE COIN

While there is truth to the statement that grief is the cost of love, it is not the whole truth. Within human relationships, there is no such thing as perfect love; rather, relationships are composed of two kinds of love, opposite sides of the same coin: love fulfilled and love unfulfilled. To avoid becoming stuck in grief, it is necessary to grieve both sides of the coin. It might help to think of it as grieving the loss of what you most appreciated about your shared love and also grieving the flaws within your shared love. Give yourself permission to be honest and know that addressing that which was unfulfilled is not a betrayal to the person who died nor is it dismissive of all that was good in the relationship.

This exercise is just about getting it out, so simple words or phrases will suffice. In the provided spaces, name or otherwise describe the aspects of fulfilled love *and* the aspects of unfulfilled love that you are grieving. This is an expression of gratitude, regret, disappointment, and joy. The lists do not need to be equal in length; remember, it's not about how much you can say, but how truthful you are. You can always come back later as more comes to mind.

Love Fulfilled　　　　**Love Unfulfilled**

Reflection

"As you consider your loss, it's good to reflect on its impact upon your spiritual life."

Faith Doesn't Erase Grief, 76

"I want to still believe in God, I do. But right now, I need to explore." This client holds a permanent place in my heart. He was wise and mature beyond his age, and when he walked into each session, he let his walls come down. Simply because of his age, even before the death of his sibling, he was at a pivotal point of life and faith, of learning who he is and what he believes; when his sibling died, the faith exploration he had put off catapulted to a nonnegotiable *right now* exercise.

The faith in which he was raised did not provide room for questions or exploration, just accepted facts. The people around him told him heaven was real but didn't allow conversation about it, and that wasn't enough for him. Now that his soul *longed* for heaven to be real so that he could have assurance of his sibling's whereabouts, he needed real answers. And his anger at God? His childhood faith had taught him praise of God over and above anything else. What was he to do with this anger? He felt his faith had let him down; his sibling's death left him with a lot of big questions instead of the peace the same beliefs appeared to give his mom. He knew the only way to keep moving, to find true comfort and hope, was to allow himself to ask the big questions and wrestle with his beliefs in a world he now saw through changed eyes. He took that exploration seriously, and by the time he ended grief counseling, he felt reconnected to his sibling and felt secure in his need to keep going.

Sometimes religion uses shame or fear to dissuade us from seeking clarity, insinuating that we will be forever cut off from the divinity we worship simply for having doubts or questions, let alone *expressing* them. The reality, though, is that a survey of one's beliefs is normal and expected in grief. A person can hold a set of beliefs about life, death, and what—if anything—comes next, but those beliefs are naturally put to the test when a significant person dies. Expect it; don't ignore or try to hide it. It is important to check in with yourself spiritually throughout the grief journey. Ignoring the pull to question or explore or express feelings of abandonment, anger, and disappointment or whatever else you might experience will trap you in your grief. Remember that grief is a whole-being experience, and that includes your faith. Go at your own pace, but give yourself space and permission to examine where you might need to go within your spiritual life.

Action Challenge

Spend some time answering the following questions, either in conversation with a trusted person or in a journal: How did this death impact what you believe about life, death, and what comes next? Do you feel less connected to God or more drawn to God, or is your faith unchanged? What big question or statement are you hesitating to say?

TOOLKIT: GUIDED FREE ASSOCIATION

Guided Free Association helps clients uncover things that need to come to the surface in order for grievers to move beyond them. In this section, the focus of the exercise is *connection*. What connection do you most need? What connection do you avoid? How can you fill the need for connection? This tool will assist you in answering these and similar questions and will help you break free from what holds you back. Read through all the steps *before* beginning so that you are prepared to move seamlessly through the process.

Step 1: Choose a Focus Word, such as "God," "loss," or "longing"—something related to the concept of connection. Your word might represent something you miss ("hugs," "walks together"); something you wish you could feel or experience ("one more," "peace," "hope"); or the absence of connection to yourself, the person, or God ("abandoned," "lost," "confused," "purpose"). Once you choose a word, write it here:

Step 2: Start a timer for fifteen to thirty seconds and stare at your Focus Word, repeating it in your mind until the timer sounds.

Step 3: Start a timer for ten to fifteen minutes and begin writing on the next page. Let your subconscious take over and allow your words to meander without intrusion. Have another sheet of paper or a laptop nearby in case you need more room.

Step 4: When the timer sounds, stop writing. Move from the space where you completed this activity and do something soothing and preferably physical. Take a shower, go for a walk, call a friend. If you want to process what you wrote, I encourage you to do so with a therapist or trusted person.

Connection

Reflection

> "It is important to note that being content might include feeling disconnected from God; that is okay!"
>
> *Faith Doesn't Erase Grief*, 77

There are moments in life when it is completely normal and acceptable to stop talking to God, even when you know it won't be permanent. That can be difficult to hear, and as an ordained minister, I will say there are circles I move in where my saying this is not well received. I keep saying it anyway because I think it is important for all believers to consider it. Here's why:

1. It's honest. Rather than feigning a relationship with God in order to meet the expectations of others, it's healthier to embrace where you are in your process. Don't hide it from God or anyone else.
2. It leaves room for change. In these times of silence, you can name both where you are and where you want to be. You can trust that when you are ready to start working things through with God, God will be there.
3. It's real. God does not desire an approach from us that is so formal it becomes false. God has drawn us into a covenanted, direct, intimate relationship that invites transparency, and because of that, you can know that God isn't going anywhere. Be assured a "time-out" will not sever the relationship.
4. It's personal. Being honest with yourself about these moments is not an expectation or invitation for others to do as you do. You get to walk your own road because you are the only one who had *your* relationship with the person who died and the only one who has *your* relationship with God. You can trust your intuition to

lead you through the phases you need as you need them; you don't need anyone else's permission or direction.

In short, no one—not your pastor or elder, not the congregant who sits next to you every week, not your neighbor or co-worker—can define your spiritual contentment. If contentment for you includes a silent pause, empower yourself to own it and to trust the experience.

Action Challenge

Jot down the primary thought that came to mind and heart as you read this Reflection. Did it resonate? Did it feel foreign or unfamiliar? Did it resonate *and* feel uncomfortable? There's no right or wrong response; just write down a few words so you have them for whenever you complete the Toolkit on the next page.

TOOLKIT: MEASURING YOUR SPIRITUAL CONTENTMENT

Part of the spiritual aspect of grief is to name where you are with God and then determine if you are content with your status or if you would like something different. This exercise is not so much about describing your relationship as it is about evaluating your contentment with it. In short, it is taking stock and setting a goal. Maybe you are already spiritually content, so your goal is to stay that way throughout your grief work. Maybe you feel disconnected from God, and the goal is to find ways to reconnect. Or maybe you recognize your current lack of spiritual connection, and you don't have a goal to regain that connection, at least for now. Whatever it is, take an honest look inside and challenge yourself to name where you are with God right now; then identify where you want to be with God later on in your grief. For a bit more context, pause and complete the preceding Reflection before returning to this Toolkit.

Date:

Today, my relationship with God/spiritual connection is . . .

My goal for my relationship with God/spiritual connection is . . .

Reflection

"When you are given a moment of connection, take it, enjoy it, feel it, and learn from it, then let it be. If you allow yourself to sit waiting for the next one, you run the risk of becoming trapped in grief and interrupting your relationship with God."
Faith Doesn't Erase Grief, 177

"I felt him lay his hand on my shoulder."
"I saw him in my windshield."
"I felt her presence in the room with me."
"I smelled their cologne."
"We talked in my dream last week."

What would you add to that list? It is important for your forward movement through grief to take these moments, visits, gifts—whatever you want to call them—at face value. If something felt good or encouraging or loving, don't steal it away from yourself by trying to analyze it logically or religiously. Just let it be.

And then, continue living.

When it has been a long time since you last felt a connection to your person, it is tempting to latch onto the experience and bring the rest of your life to a complete halt, braced and eager as you are for the next rendezvous. I get it. I do. I have experienced connections in the forms of dreams and visions, and I know how wonderful it feels to see them and talk with them and hear their voice again. But as good as it feels, and as much as we want to, we cannot stay there, because we need to continue living in the present and moving toward the future. That is why the dreams, visions, scents, movements of air, and pressure on the skin are so fleeting.

I believe God gives these gifts of connection to provide us some respite, a deep breath, and a resurgence of motivation to keep going. To dwell indefinitely in an experience of connection, only awaiting the next one, however, is dangerous. It will quickly result in stagnation and disconnect from the world around you, it will trap you in the past, and, if you stay in that place too long, you might forget how to live. This is one of the many both/and realities of grief. Try to remain open to these connections because you never know when you will be gifted one, *and* while you wait, continue working through your grief with the set intention of moving forward.

Action Challenge

Capture your moments of connection in a collection you can revisit. Write out what happened or record yourself explaining it so that you have something to go back to.

If you have not yet had an encounter like those described, ask yourself if you are open to receiving it. If you aren't, that is okay; everyone's grief needs are different. If you are, know that it is also okay to ask God for that gift. You might write a prayer or a note to the person who died specifically about this type of connection and explain your hopes. Entrust the prayer to the Spirit and express your commitment to keep living even while you expectantly wait.

TOOLKIT: PSALM WRITING

Psalms are tools of expression that give words to situations we otherwise cannot describe. We often overlook the fact that the psalmists were seeking a way to process both their own situations and God's role within them. I think psalms are included in the Bible not just to give us poetry to illustrate a multitude of scenarios but also to remind us to use the same process for the same reason.

To begin, find a few psalms that echo your current emotions, and look for similarities between them. Where does God fit in? How are emotions expressed? Then either personalize one of the psalms you just read or write your own using the same structure and techniques you observed. To personalize a psalm, simply replace the words that do not fit your situation with words that do. For example, if a psalm is mostly a good fit for a health situation, but it uses too many warlike words and images, remove those and replace them with words like "cancer," "health," "medical system," or "treatment room." To write your own psalm, simply imitate the ones you've studied. Do they open with lament, with accusation, with supplication? Do they use repetition for emphasis, physical details to express emotion? Use whatever works for you.

Remember, no one is judging the final product. The purpose here is to provide a different outlet for your processing and expression. Try to shake off any self-consciousness before you begin, and invite the Spirit to accompany you as you work.

Reflection

"The life of faith is not a life free of darkness."
Faith Doesn't Erase Grief, 97

"*Likewise the Spirit helps us in our weakness; for we do not know how to pray as we ought, but that very Spirit intercedes with sighs too deep for words.*"
Romans 8:26, NRSV

Sometimes the darkness is too much to bear, so thick it prevents any ability to dredge up the words or even the will to pray. Faith has never equaled the absence of darkness, and that will remain true until an unknown time. Though it can be nice to wonder about and contemplate the hope of that time, there are depths of darkness through which the light of that "one day" cannot penetrate.

I have been in those depths and know what it is to feel a genuine inability to pray, and not for any lack of words. In such depths, we might also lack the will, the desire to reach out to God. Whether from feeling abandoned or unheard or unseen by God or from exhaustion over prayers poured out and unanswered, there simply are times when we don't feel like praying. In those times, the Spirit joins us in the dark and intercedes on our behalf.

Did you notice in the opening verse just how the Spirit intercedes? Not with words; not with correction or admonishment; not with shame or judgment. No, the Spirit intercedes with *sighs* that convey more than human words ever could. Through the Spirit our needs are poured out before God in a language God deeply understands.

This intercession might not lift you up immediately, and it might not remove the fullness of the pain. It may do those things, but it might not. What this work of the Spirit *does* offer is the reassurance that you remain connected to God, even when words fail. If you are unable to take comfort from that right now, that is okay. If you can receive it as comfort, allow it to infuse you. There is no pressure to change anything. Just allow yourself to lean in, and let the Spirit do what the Spirit does.

Action Challenge

Jesus sent us the Spirit to be our advocate throughout this journey called life, and the Spirit does so with and without our awareness. Becoming aware of the Spirit's presence in your life, however, does something to your own spirit. For the next week, spend a few minutes each day attuning yourself to the Spirit. Find a time to be still in silence, and listen with all your senses. You may find you are not as alone as you felt before.

Next Level

Record, with the date, what you experience in each of your listening sessions; then set a reminder on your phone to return to the practice in another month or two. Compare the two experiences, reflecting on how your sense of the Spirit has changed (or not).

TOOLKIT: PSALM 42

The poetry that comprises the book of Psalms gives us words to explain feelings or situations we are otherwise unable to articulate, so it is important to reflect on what occurs within you as you read it. To practice this, read Psalm 42 in several translations (you can find multiple versions online). Take your time with it as you ingest the words. If you find yourself racing through or skimming the surface, go back to the start and try again. Read with an open heart and mind. After you've read through the psalm at least three times, proceed to the next step.

Complete the following sentence starters with the *first* response that comes to mind. Try not to edit your response or change it. Just release whatever your subconscious brings up.

The dominant feeling I had while reading this psalm was . . .

When I read the phrase "my soul thirsts for God," I . . .

To me, the words "Hope in God, for I shall again praise God" express. . .

The verse I most disagreed with is . . .

The verse that most resonated with me is . . .

I hope . . .

Once you've completed the sentence starters, capture any additional reflections or reactions before ending your grief work for the day.

Reflection

"We grieve because we love, and loving others is the DNA God implanted in us. To avoid relationships out of fear is to deprive the self of connection, which is one of the most basic needs we have."

Faith Doesn't Erase Grief, 193

Depending on how you are working your way through this guide, that quote might feel like a bit of déjà vu. This same quote is used in a different section, viewed there from the *through* lens; here we look at it from the *connection* lens.

"She was my best friend. She held all my secrets, and now I'm left holding hers. She knew me long before I met my husband! It's like she was an anchor I didn't know I had, and now that she's not here, I don't know what to do."

The fear of opening the heart back up to relationships, old and new alike, is real and born from pain. Though that client had been prepared for her best friend's death, she was stunned by the impact it left behind, an impact that included a felt inability to *ever* again invest in that type of friendship. When she started her grief work, that attitude made sense. In Early Grief, and into Middle Grief, the pain of physical absence is so prevalent that the flip side of that coin—the fullness that derives from connection—is impossible to imagine.

My client worked hard, though, and eventually arrived at a session feeling torn. She had a solid continued connection to her best friend and was grateful for it, but she had started to also feel a desire to reinvest in friendships with the living. Together we worked through her feelings of betrayal and fear that her best friend would resent her for cultivating other friendships. Then we worked on her reluctance to go deeper with her other friends even as they poured into her. Eventually, with persistence and honesty, she came to understand the natural need within all of us—even the most introverted among us—to connect with others. She realized avoiding connection with others for fear of losing it in the future was only causing her more pain in the present. No one would ever replace her best friend, yet in recognizing her inherent need for connection, she gave herself the gift of the possibility of *another* best friend.

Action Challenge

Is there a relationship you have stopped nurturing since this death of your loved one? Challenge yourself to take a step, just one step, toward reinvesting in it. The next time you are invited to a meal or other activity, accept. You can put boundaries in place such as saying yes to dinner but no to the movie, but do consider trying to reengage. Trying sends the message that you have not forgotten about these other people, while boundaries remind them that, while you work through grief, reinvesting is on your terms. Alternatively, if you know you're not yet ready to accept an invitation, text or mail a card just to let them know you're thinking of them.

TOOLKIT: SEARCH FOR THE TRINKET

> "Continue living and trusting that on the other side of each grief wave is the opportunity to think about your person in a way you might not have for some time."
>
> *Faith Doesn't Erase Grief,* 151

Grief waves are beasts, unwelcome and undesired emotional gut punches; they are also inevitable. As with all other aspects of grief, it is a futile, significant waste of precious energy to fight them, so the remaining option is to accept them. Remember, acceptance is not the same as saying, "Yippee! Another grief wave!" while you dance in celebration, nor is it an admittance of defeat. Acceptance is simply acknowledging that grief waves are going to happen and deciding you are not going to put life on pause because they do. You are not a surfer in the ocean just floating around for the next set of waves. You have a life to live, so you can determine not to allow grief waves to be more of an interruption to your life than they are naturally.

The start of a grief wave is usually something that hits at least one of the five senses and, oftentimes beyond your conscious awareness, triggers a memory that floods your system. To embrace these waves—to foster the acceptance of their sheer existence—it helps to seek what I call a Trinket on the back side of the wave. This might be a memory from a time in the person's life that you haven't thought about since they died. It might be a smile that forms even as tears fall while you experience your special song for the first time without them. The Trinket is a piece of them that you get back.

Use the following questions to help you process the wave and sift out the Trinkets.

What did you see/taste/hear/feel/smell just before the wave?

What memory or memories come to mind when you recall what you experienced just before the wave?

What lingering emotion is with you after the wave?

TOOLKIT: TRAJECTORY TRACKER 2

This tool reflects the fact that grief is not steady, linear, predictable, or unidirectional. Here the adage of "one step forward, two steps back" does not apply, though it might feel like it does. The Trajectory Tracker is here to help you in this confusing reality to visualize where you are and where you want to be. Be sure to date a trajectory when you complete it so you can later compare it to others. Hopefully in this way, over time, you will clearly see that you have moved forward overall. If you compare the completed trackers and find that you have *not* moved forward, consider that an indicator you should reach out for more help.

On the next page you will see an image of a path with three main areas: Start, Middle, and Beyond. *Start* indicates the place or time when your thoughts and actions are stuck in the past, with minimal participation in the present and no thoughts of the future. *Middle* signals a shift to a state where you are living more in the present, able both to remember the past without getting caught up in it and to envision the future. *Beyond* is the final stage of the path where you now fully participate in daily life and actively work on building toward the future. You have learned how to carry your loved one's presence with you as you desire and to control when to reflect and remember.

Considering those three main areas, reflect on where you are in the present moment. Are you close to the start, firmly in the middle, or somewhere between? Place a mark along the pathway, indicating the date, to show where you think you are at this point, and add a few comments or sentences about why you placed yourself there. Then write a goal for where you want to be when you complete the next tracker.

Date:

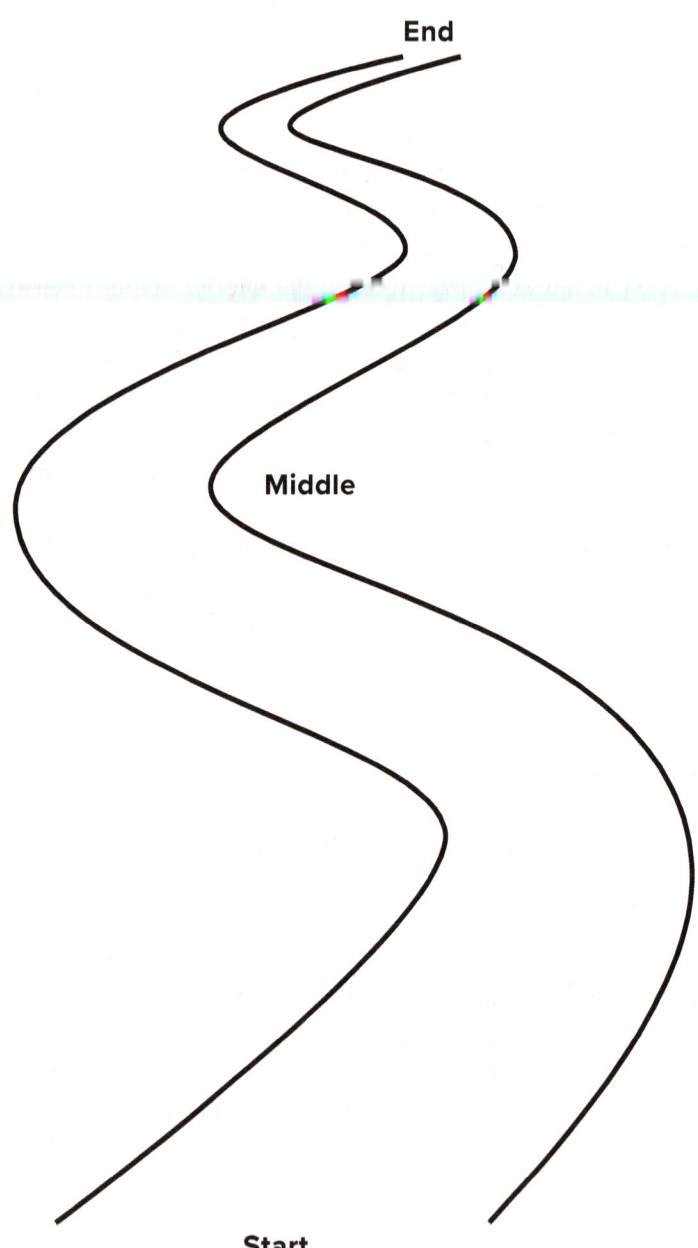

Identity

Think about how the three phases of grief—Early Grief, Middle Grief, and Lasting Grief—vary in their focus. In Early Grief the focus is almost entirely on the past with minimal awareness of the present. In Middle Grief the focus expands to incorporate more of the present while some lingering in the past continues, though this lessens. The transition from Middle Grief to Lasting Grief is marked by the restored ability to live almost entirely in the present *and* to envision the future, changed though it may be, and all with the assurance that the past is there for you in the form of memories whenever you need them.

For most grievers, it is not until they are well into Middle Grief that the ability to focus more on the present translates into contemplation of their own identity—meaning how they understand themselves in their new reality. It might be, then, that you do not feel drawn to this section until later in your grief journey. It is okay if the first several times you flip to this section you are not yet ready to think about who you were, who you are, and what you might look forward to in your changed future. *This is your permission to not force it.* You will know when you are ready to begin hoping and dreaming again; trust that it will happen when it should.

Reshaping identity—labels, beliefs, goals, hopes, dreams,

plans, and desires—after the death of a significant person is good, difficult work. I want to highlight for you, especially if you are wondering whether now is the time to start this section, that part of identity work is naming and releasing what you do *not* want to take forward into your changed future. You do not owe anything to the person who died. Changing plans, labels, roles, and so on is not a betrayal of them, nor does it signify a diminished love or a lower quality relationship. Instead, it displays the deepest level of acceptance of your new reality and is a significant step toward reengaging in life.

To most benefit from the Toolkit and Reflection pages here, please take your time. You might find that you work in this section in fits and starts, or you might turn a corner and suddenly feel ready to tackle everything, leaving aside all other sections until you complete this one. With the other three sections, I encourage you to dip in and out of them as needed, but this section is different. If you dive in too soon, you might become discouraged at your inability to complete the exercises, and you might feel unable to benefit from the Reflections. Wait until you are ready—I promise, you'll know. Then, when you are, tackle the section in whatever manner best fits your situation. If you need to begin only with releasing portions of your identity, do so. If a balance of letting go and dreaming is better, take that route. You are never locked in; listen to your intuition and go at your own pace.

TOOLKIT: OBJECT LESSON

If you had to illustrate your grief, what would it look like? The image that most resonates with me is that of a large internal ball with sharp edges that poke and prod, inflicting pain from head to toe when I move. Then, as I work at it, it slowly shrinks in size, and the spikes fall off. Draw what your grief looks like and how you carry it in your body. Is it all-consuming? Maybe it's on the smaller side, so that it bounces around your body? Are its edges, sharp, dull, or some of each? Is it small enough that you can keep it in one place, tucked away where it causes minimal pain? Draw (or describe with words if that's more of your thing) what is true of you and your grief right now, and record the date.

Reflection

> "Who you are as a beloved child of God is something permanently protected from the masked burglar of grief."
>
> *Faith Doesn't Erase Grief*, 11

In 2023 musician Andy Grammer released "I Need a New Money," a spoken word track that reflects on how things might change if we judged ourselves and others based not on the money we make but on how we live. In the chorus he states, "I need a new money that measures my inherent value." A thesaurus offers to replace "inherent" with "innate," "inborn," and "natural" and "value" with "worth," "importance," and "significance," which results in alternate phrases like "natural worth," "inborn importance," or, my favorite, "innate significance."

Of all that the Grief Thief takes, the most vulnerable is the belief that you are a beloved child of God. Period. No matter what you do, no matter your questions or doubts, God knowing you as a child is innate to your identity. It cannot be taken from you.

There is a lot of identity work in grief. The death of a family member results in a changed family system, including new, changed, or removed roles within that system. The death of a friend leads to reflection on who that friend helped you to become, and it might lead you to evaluate whether you still possess those qualities after their death. From a young age we learn to define ourselves by our jobs, status, family, and relationships. When a death changes any of those things, it can feel disorienting and all-consuming, making it difficult to find an anchor that sustains us through even the largest waves.

The work of grief necessitates your review, release, and reclaiming of various identities as you come to know who you are now. As you embark on that process, know that your identity as God's own is innate and immovable. It isn't going anywhere and cannot be changed, not even by death. Rest in the security of that truth.

Action Challenge

What does it mean to find your identity in Christ? The answers to this varies among the branches of Christianity and according to the multitude of Bible translations, but what is most important here is *your* understanding of this piece of your identity. Take time now to define what it means to *you* to be permanently identified as Christ's own. Safety and security? Inherent value? Peace in the chaos? Write it out in only a sentence or two, and if you are feeling ambitious, list a few biblical references that help support this sense of your identity for when you need a reminder.

TOOLKIT: 1 CORINTHIANS 13

Note: If engaging this passage of scripture is too much for you today, that's okay. Skip it and come back further down the road.

1 Corinthians 13 is a passage that is most often used to define love between two people. It can also be used to improve love of self, which is an important aspect of knowing and embracing your identity. To that end, listed here are some words that follow the phrase "love is" throughout the opening verses. Take your time with each word, writing down how you can extend love to *yourself* after each prompt. To take it deeper, add how loving yourself helps you better know yourself. If this exercise is useful to you, I encourage you to complete the same process for the rest of the "love is" words and phrases in 1 Corinthians 13.

Patient

Kind

Not Rude

Hopes All Things

Never Ends

Reflection

> "For I am convinced that neither death, nor life . . . nor anything else in all creation, will be able to separate us from the love of God in Christ Jesus our Lord." Romans 8:38–39, NRSV

The purpose of this guidebook is not to delve into theology; rather, it is to assist grieving believers with the understanding that God desires for them to do the work of grief, not pretend it does not exist. Therefore, we will examine this passage through the lens of grief. As discussed elsewhere in this guidebook, the work of grief might result in the need for a break from God. If this Reflection is one of your first, know that this subtheme is a thread that connects all four sections because this one truth is too often either overlooked or condemned.

While we logically know that all life ends in death, that knowledge does not eliminate the pain, anger, despair, and trauma of death, and sometimes those reactions are so consuming that remaining in active relationship with God while trying to sort through them is not possible. This is okay, and today's verses from Romans 8 will remind you of that truth when you question it. You see, no matter where you need to go, God's love goes with you. It cannot be stripped away by silence. It cannot be stripped away by anger. It cannot be stripped away by distance. It cannot be stripped away by exploration. According to Paul, nothing natural—or even supernatural—is enough to remove God's love from you.

So while you work to reconcile yourself to the fact that your person died and you need to somehow continue living without their physical presence, if you need to step away from God to do so, rest assured that God understands and will not leave you. You two can talk about it later. God will be there when you are ready. In fact, no matter where you go, God will be there still because that's how far God's love goes. It cannot be outrun or destroyed beyond repair.

Go where you need to go, say what you need to say, do

what you need to do—without causing harm to yourself or others—and do so with confidence that God loves you still.

Action Challenge

Read the whole of Romans 8:38–39 and Psalm 139:1–18, preferably in a few different translations. What do you hear God saying to you about your grief journey at this moment?

Next Level

Choose a verse or two from those listed in the Action Challenge that strongly resonate with you and rewrite them to reflect your story in this moment. Date this exercise and commit to doing it again in a few months to track what changes.

TOOLKIT: GET IT OUT THERE

There is a lot of discussion in this guidebook about pouring everything out before God, but talking about it and engaging the practice are not the same. This exercise kickstarts the actual practice with ease. Below are a few sentence starters that attempt to get at things many grievers feel the desire, but not the freedom, to say to God. Do one a day, one a month, or all in one sitting. Grab an extra sheet of paper or have something near to hand where you can write more responses if you run out of room (or just don't want the answers on this page). The most important part of this process is to respond with the *first words* that come to mind. No editing for content or language. Just get it out: It is one of the most important ways to help you move forward. You and God can sort it out later if needed.

I can't believe you . . .

My faith in you is . . .

When I hear songs of praise I . . .

You could have intervened. You didn't, and . . .

I long to . . .

Where is/are . . .

What is my . . .

Reflection

"Grief changes you. It's inevitable."
Faith Doesn't Erase Grief, 103

It is impossible to escape grief unchanged. The brain creates new pathways. We feel newly complex emotions and develop new passions. We view relationships differently. We view ourselves differently. Here's what you need to remember: These changes might be inevitable, but they are not bad.

Change can be painful and can even result in grief as you work through the associated losses, such as the loss of purpose or identity that can come with retirement. Yet if you do a bit of life review, I imagine you'll find many examples of times you found something worth celebrating on the other side of a difficult change. In the same way, you will not—cannot—be the person you were prior to the death, but that does not mean it's all bad. It does not mean you are no longer you.

Each person has core inherent traits—some that are shared across humanity, and some that are unique to each individual—that cannot be stolen from you no matter how many times the Grief Thief strikes. We all also have traits and likes and hobbies and desires and dislikes that fluctuate throughout our lives. Have you ever noticed that you choose relationships (both friendships and romantic relationships) based on commonalities between you and other people? In long-term relationships, that shared foundation must be regularly adjusted and gradually built throughout life as we grow and change alongside each other. It is similarly remodeled by grief.

As you progress through your grief, take inventory of both your inherent traits and your absorbed traits—those traits you've developed or picked up from another person—and consider what serves you well and what you want to release. What did your person help foster in you? Do you want to continue with that, or did you take that on simply because of your relationship with that person? Perhaps you never golfed a day in your life until you met them, and you realized early in the relationship that you had to choose between golfing or decreased time with them. Perhaps you learned to golf just to stay close to them and even enjoyed it at times. Strange as it may seem, one way to get to know yourself through grief is to decide, for example, whether you have any desire to continue golfing or if you'd rather leave the greens behind. Never picking up another club is not a betrayal of your person. It does not diminish the times you spent playing rounds together, and it in no way invalidates the good memories you made while golfing. All it means is that you started the hobby to spend more time with them, and now, with the absence of their physical presence, it is not something that you want to continue.

The changes you experience in grief will vary in scope and weight, but you do not need to fear them. Face them. Investigate them. Embrace what you want to embrace, and release the rest.

Action Challenge

Is there something you feel *obligated* to continue but do not *want* to continue? Allow yourself time to reflect on that, or talk it through with a trusted person. If you decide to let it go, create a ritual to say goodbye. Tell the deceased why you no longer want to continue that activity, and thank them for bringing it into your life for a season.

TOOLKIT: I AM

Write out as many "I am" statements as you can think of. You can highlight roles (familial, professional, community, church, etc.), beliefs, identities, passions, loves; there are no wrong answers. Do not give it a lot of thought—just list as many as you can.

Now circle the "I am" statements that you believe are God-implanted—natural, core truths of who *you are*. Then, erase or cross out anything you want to release because it was yours only for a season, and leave alone anything about which you remain undecided. Before you end your grief work today, decide how you can ensure that the things you circled stay as a permanent part of your identity.

TOOLKIT: A LOVE LETTER TO YOURSELF

It is easy to lose sight of yourself in grief, especially if you are simultaneously caring for others. Today, write yourself a letter. It can be a letter of love and encouragement, a letter in which you extend yourself grace or forgiveness, a letter of commitment to your hopes or dreams, a letter of release, or anything else that resonates with you. If you struggle to settle on a topic, spend a few moments looking through the other pages you have completed so far in this guidebook, particularly within this section, and pay attention to what stirs up inside you as you do. Allow that to inform the purpose of your letter.

A powerful bonus step: take a picture of the letter you've just written and schedule an email to yourself with the picture attached. Or copy the letter, seal it in a self-addressed stamped envelope, and ask someone to mail it to you in a few months. I won't be offended if you tear out this page and mail it; go for it if that's easiest.

Reflection

> "You are an individual with your own personality, and you are the only one who had your relationship with the deceased, so looking to someone else's grief experience to understand your own is futile."
>
> *Faith Doesn't Erase Grief*, 37

"I talked with my mom and my sister a lot this week. They're really struggling, and I just need to help them. I sent each of them the workbook I've been using too." When my client started her session this way, my heart sank; it sank further when I asked what work *she'd* done in her workbook and she couldn't answer me. All her available time for grief work had been spent on others.

On the surface, what she did was a great service to her family. But beneath the surface, my client used those conversations for two additional reasons other than helping. First, they let her learn how others were working through their grief process, and second, they let her avoid doing her own grief work. Service to others, planning what to do instead of doing it, even learning about grief—these are all actions that are indeed purposeful and *appear* healthy. Unfortunately, when used to consistently push off actually *doing* the grief work, these actions become distractions that only serve to delay the necessary and inevitable. They are also hidden comparison traps. Reading books about grief or talking to people who are grieving the same person about *their* process does serve you, but only to a point. If you take it too far, listening to other people's experiences can cause you to miss out on your own work.

There's a phrase from the SAT prep episode of my favorite teen drama that, strangely, summarizes how to avoid getting stuck in a grief comparison trap: "Scan, discard, select, move on." Whatever helpful tool or process a friend might rave about or whatever tool you read about in the latest book, it is not going to be an automatic fit for *you* and *your* grief work. Instead of assuming anything and everything is beneficial, apply that process. Scan the tool. Does it fit with how *you* process information? Does it suit your skills and interests? Since your relationship with the deceased was unique to the two of you, consider if the tool you are contemplating fully addresses the needs of your grief journey. If the answer is no, discard it, and if the answer is yes, select it. Then move on: Proceed with the work itself. Leave behind anything you discard and put into practice everything you select.

It is good to fill your grief toolbox with a variety of equipment, especially because what works for today's grief wave might not work for tomorrow's. But your chosen tools need to be a good fit for you. Do not waste time contorting yourself to fit the tool; modify the tool to suit you.

Action Challenge

Create a list of up to five categories to reference when choosing if what you hear, watch, see, or read about will benefit your grief work. Do you prefer creative expression, writing, or observing? How do you put what you learn into practice? Examples of labels you can use to sort and select your grief work tools might include words like "short," "artistic," "active," "intellectual," "emotional," "instructive," and "open-ended." Remember, don't spend so much time on it that this exercise becomes a distraction from the actual work of grief. Identify the tools that best fit your personality, how you learn, and what you like to do; then put them to work!

TOOLKIT: PARALLEL SHIFTS

"In relationships... lives and interests become intertwined to the point that when one part of the relationship is no longer physically present, it becomes unimaginable to return to that activity, place, or even food ever again. This is why parallel shifts are so beneficial: they represent something new you can do on your own yet remain tied to key parts of yourself that your person helped foster in you."

Faith Doesn't Erase Grief, 104

A parallel shift[2] is simply a new activity that provides the same benefit as an activity you have struggled to resume since the person's death. See the following examples and then use the rest of the page to note your current hobbies and any possible parallel shifts they could take. As you try out potential shifts, come back to this page and note the ones that work well for you. Lastly, know that many people are able to return to the formerly enjoyed activity after getting back into the groove through the use of these parallel shifts.

Past Activity	Parallel Shift Possibilities
Running	swimming, Rollerblading, kickboxing, weightlifting
Knitting	crocheting, painting, diamond painting, sewing

---

2. For more context and examples of parallel shifts, see pages 102–104 in *Faith Doesn't Erase Grief*.

Reflection

> "The early believers understood that to honor Jesus they needed to use their own unique personal gifts and talents to continue the spirit of the work Jesus began. The same is true for us today. It is well and good to continue a piece of your person's story, but do so with your skills, your perspective, and your personality."
>
> *Faith Doesn't Erase Grief*, 160

There is a subtle yet crucial nuance between doing something in honor of someone and continuing someone's work. You and the person who died are not the same. Even the life experiences you shared were experienced differently, which is something to be celebrated—that's what keeps relationships interesting, right? It brings richness to companionship to discuss things you enjoy together, whether for the same reasons or not. Sadly, this also means you cannot continue their work and expect it to turn out the same as it was. You are not them, so it is futile to try to re-create their actions. This is no failure on your part, nor are you in any way disappointing your person. Read that again. What you can do, however, is take the pieces of you that retain interest in what you shared with them and continue in their honor. Not to replicate the former experience, but to continue it into a new phase, to grow it and possibly mold it into something more reflective of who *you* are even as it retains their imprint.

Note the phrase "shared with them" too. This is as crucial as the nuance of honoring versus continuing. No matter the number of people who say, "They would want you to," you are not obligated to continue what they started if it is not right *for you*. It is not a betrayal to them. It does not suggest that you stopped loving them. It honors your need to continue living and moving forward, and you can trust they respect that healthy choice.

Jesus called each of his followers because they had distinct personalities and gifts, and through their years together, Jesus showed each of them how to embrace his teachings in their own unique way. When he died, they knew Jesus did not expect them to do exactly what he did but rather to continue in the spirit of what he taught. They couldn't replicate Jesus's actions, and they knew that to try would be exhausting and destructive. Instead, they each went forward and spread the gospel in the ways that fit their individual personalities. And you know what? That is precisely what Jesus wanted.

There are many ways to honor the person who died without changing the direction of your life and doing something that does not resonate with your soul. Whatever changes you make, make them because they are right for *you* (and your family, if applicable).

Action Challenge

If you feel pressure to continue a project or other work that belonged to the deceased, take a few moments to reflect on that pressure. Determine if the project is meaningful *to you*, if it is something you have the bandwidth to take on, or if it is something that meant a lot to them but not so much to you personally. With this information, you can decide on next steps that honor your person *and* are in line with who you are created to be.

TOOLKIT: HORIZON LINE

"The road of grief is often like hiking in a sand dune. It is long and challenging with no indication of relief. But as you near the water, you feel a breeze, and you come over the final hill to something unexpected and beautiful. The horizon greets you with a promise of continued life, *renewed purpose*, and the hope that you will carry your loved one with you into your next adventure."

Faith Doesn't Erase Grief, 41, emphasis added

This Toolkit activity is found in three sections, each with a slightly different emphasis depending on the theme of that section. Today consider what your horizon might look like as it relates to new or updated dreams, goals, and/or understanding of your purpose in life. What is in the foreground? What awaits you out in the distance? What is the promise beyond the horizon? If you connect with the sand dune image in the opening quote, ask yourself if you're still climbing the dune or cresting it with a close view of the water. Do you prefer a desert scene, or perhaps a cityscape? Reread the opening quote, listen to what stirs in your heart and mind, and draw that below. If drawing intimidates you, that's okay! Use colors or words around the provided horizon line to create an image in your mind in whatever way works for you.

Reflection

"When Martha heard that Jesus was coming, she went and met him, while Mary stayed at home."
John 11:20, NRSV

"Grief changed you, yes; but nothing can change who you are at your core."
Faith Doesn't Erase Grief, 11

Lazarus, Mary, and Martha were siblings, and they were also Jesus's friends. They knew him before he began his official ministry, and they followed him when that time came; in short, they knew his heart, and they believed in his miracles. Because of their close, long-term relationship with him, when Mary and Martha saw their brother dying, they sent word to Jesus, hoping and trusting that he had a miracle ready for Lazarus.

Jesus did not arrive when the sisters believed and trusted he would. In fact, Lazarus was already entombed by the time Jesus arrived. The sisters had requested his help not only as a dear friend but as their teacher and leader—and he showed up too late. Yet even though they both asked for Jesus and both endured their brother's death without him, when they found out Jesus was finally approaching, only Martha left to meet him, and Mary stayed home. Why?

Because Martha was not Mary and Mary was not Martha. They were individuals who each coped with situations in their own unique ways. Even in the throes of early grief, their personalities shone through. And perhaps what I love most about this passage is that Jesus met each of them in their individual grief, with no expectation of anything different.

There is no denying that grief changes people. It can bring clarity, inspire new passions, lead to reevaluation of relationships and choices, leave us restless for change, and invoke deep reflection. What it cannot do is change who you are at your core: that which is uniquely you, implanted in you as a created being with your own purpose.

Getting back to a past reality is a false goal of grief. Your world has changed; it cannot be what it was. Yet even still, you can continue growing into who you are meant to be. That anchor in your soul is not gone. It might be difficult to feel. You might not want to see it right now. All of that is okay. Know that when you are ready, the anchor of who you truly are will be there to center you and help you reestablish your footing.

Because of who she was at her core, Martha needed the reassurance of her Messiah. She'd trusted her friend and teacher to save her brother's life; when he died instead, she was lost. To find her way, it wasn't her friend she needed, but her teacher. She wanted to be shown how and where she could still find hope. Mary didn't need a theological discussion with the teacher. What she needed was the opportunity to openly express her frustration, disbelief, anger, and sadness that Jesus didn't do what she knew he could have done. She needed the sympathetic ear of a friend. These were two different women with different personalities who needed different things from Jesus, and he gave them each what they needed. That is how he loved them in their grief, and how he loves you in yours.

Action Challenge

Imagine receiving the news that Jesus is on his way to your house. What would you do? How would you react? Would you speak to him? If so, what would you say? Before the end of today, whatever you imagined, do it. Say it, shout it, cry it, fall into his arms, stomp off. Do what you need to do and trust that whatever you need from God, you'll receive.

Reflection

> *"Then Job arose, tore his robe, shaved his head, and fell on the ground and worshipped."*
>
> Job 1:20 NRSV

> "For Job, not losing the faith he had was as essential as continuing to breathe. To him faith was his only chance of surviving the unimaginable."
>
> *Faith Doesn't Erase Grief*, 119

When my client's mother called me, she had two goals for his counseling. The first goal was to give him space to talk about his grief after witnessing the sudden death of a friend. As a teenager, he was experiencing just how varied grief reactions could be, and his parents, rightly so, wanted to give him an outlet to explore his grief without judgment or interference from others. His mother phrased her second goal like this: "His dad and I want to make sure he still believes in God when he comes through this."

The fact that she voiced this told me, without my ever even meeting him, that her son was struggling spiritually with the death of his friend. It also told me that he was likely okay with his struggling, while his parents obviously were not. I made it clear to his mom that the only guarantee I could give her was that I would create intentional space for him to explore his beliefs and, if he was agreeable, would help him grieve within a Christian framework. The rest was up to him and the Spirit.

Then, because the therapeutic relationship is dependent on trust, I told him of his parents' goal at our first session. I assured him that while they had stipulated it to me, this was still his time, and he would be safe in our sessions to explore, or not explore, what he needed.

The phase of spiritual development in which a person determines if the faith of their parents aligns with their personal beliefs typically occurs in early adulthood when they leave their childhood home, but because of the unexpected death of his friend, my client was thrust into that phase early at only fifteen years old. He had been raised to believe in a God who has control over everything and the power to do anything, yet his friend had still died. My client was understandably lost: The God he knew had let him down, and the world as he knew it no longer existed. As deeply as the biblical Job needed the anchor point of his faith, my client needed to explore and ask questions of a God who had become a stranger.

Job's world disappeared in an instant, and when my client's friend suddenly died, his faith as he knew it also disappeared. Job openly grieved and then worshipped. My client grieved quietly and explored his beliefs. Each individual remained true to their spiritual identity, and doing so allowed them both to move through grief in a healthy way.

Action Challenge

Write down your faith goal for grief. Regardless of where you and God were before the person died or where you are right now, where do you want to end up? How far are you from that right now? What are the steps you can discern to reach your faith goal? Write out your answers and keep them somewhere you can easily reference them. If you feel comfortable, share them with someone who will journey with you from a place of safety, respect, and grace.

TOOLKIT: ANCHOR

Throughout this guidebook, the concept of an anchor is couched in spiritual terms related to faith. Here, though, I introduce a slightly different approach and suggest you think of it in terms of the center point of your identity. Your subsequent answers might be spiritual, but they do not need to be.

To begin, answer these questions: No matter what goes on around you, to you, or within you, what stays the same? What keeps you anchored and assures you that you will not be lost? Fill the anchor with your answers. Throw the words in as they come to you, and then, if you so desire, zhuzh up the anchor with color, added details, or the like when you are done. When the waves of grief are particularly high or strong, use this page as a reminder that, impossible though it might seem, the deepest parts of you are not going anywhere.

Reflection

> "Conversely, always trying to stay happy for the sake of positivity and ignoring other natural reactions can result in you feeling like a fraud."
>
> *Faith Doesn't Erase Grief*, 51

"As far as they are concerned, you are never having a bad day." This is a phrase that was routinely shared by my supervisor when I first started working in hospice care. In that scenario, I understand what they meant, at least theoretically, but such a practice of hiding emotions tends to spill over into all areas of life. If I were to keep the charade going long enough, I might even maintain the mask at home.

The problem with hiding emotions is at least twofold: First, you cannot *positive away* the grief. If you learned anything in the Emotions section, I feel confident it would be that the only way to truly free yourself from emotions is to *express* them. Masquerading around as if they do not exist will only work for a time. Second, the more you present an outward appearance that is incongruous with your true state, the more difficult it becomes to know what really *is* true. When that happens, you add feeling like a fraud to an already difficult situation.

There are already so many challenges in grief that result in your not feeling like yourself. Please be kind enough to yourself to reflect the truth, both to yourself and to others. To be clear, this does not mean you need to be transparent 24/7. It is still okay to power through the grocery store and hold in the breakdown until you are safely back at home, or at least in your car.

We know we need to honor our emotions, but there are times when we worry about ruining someone else's good time by showing them our current emotional reality. The impulse in those moments is to put on a happy face, but it is so draining to maintain that facade. Instead, consider a few different options:

- **Make soft plans.** In other words, until the grief waves lessen in frequency, do not fully commit to events. When you are interested in an event, tell the people who invite you that you want and intend to participate, but until the day or even the hour of an event, you can't guarantee you'll make it.
- **Give yourself permission to leave.** Perhaps the most honest thing you can do for yourself is to try and attend the experience for a limited, preset amount of time. This is a good self-compromise when you feel torn between staying at home and being with other people.
- **Stay neutral.** You do not need to fake a laugh, and you also do not need to throw negative energy into the space. If you want to stay because you need the company, but you can't match the emotional tone of those around you, allow yourself to simply absorb the vibes without fully engaging.

Action Challenge

You do not owe other people your full, true emotional experience, but you deserve to own it completely for yourself. Create a ritual or practice of a nightly self-check-in during which you reflect on the times that day when you put on a mask. Go back to those moments in your mind, remove the mask, and observe yourself as you were underneath the mask. See yourself as you were in those moments, and from a place free of reservation or judgment, allow yourself the freedom to express those emotions.

TOOLKIT: GUIDED FREE ASSOCIATION

As mentioned several places in this book, Guided Free Association is a tool to help clients uncover those things that need to come to the surface in order to move beyond them. In this section, the focus of the exercise is *identity*. Are you unsure of who you are now? Is there a part of your identity that frustrates or saddens you, or perhaps causes anxiety? What piece of your identity do you want to reclaim or relinquish? This tool will assist you in answering these and similar questions and in breaking free from whatever is keeping you stuck. Read through all the steps *before* beginning so that you are prepared to move seamlessly through the process.

Step 1: Choose a Focus Word related to your identity and write it here (e.g., "me," "one day," "home," "job," "relationship," "change"):

Step 2: Start a timer for fifteen to thirty seconds and stare at your Focus Word, repeating it in your mind until the timer sounds.

Step 3: Start a timer for ten to fifteen minutes and begin writing. Let your intuition take over, allowing your words to meander wherever they want to go. Have another sheet of paper or a laptop nearby in case you need more room for your thoughts.

Step 4: When the timer sounds, stop writing. Move from the space where you completed this activity and do something soothing and preferably physical. Take a shower, go for a walk, call a friend. If you want to process what you wrote, I encourage you to do so with a therapist or a trusted friend.

Reflection

> "But we are not meant to live in grief 24/7/365 for the remainder of life; instead, we need to be able to find a way to continue growing and becoming the people we are created to be."
>
> *Faith Doesn't Erase Grief*, 36

In the early stretch of grief, its all-consuming nature is welcome; this is an excuse to live in it. Like the permission from a rainy day to stay inside cozied up with a book, the "grief suit," as we'll call it, grants a permissive feeling to dwell in the awareness of the death, to stay in that moment for as long as the griever desires. This is something non-grievers do not get, isn't it? When you're grieving, it feels better to stay in the thick of it because you sense your loved one is there too, and to leave behind the grief suit means leaving them. Sure, to the non-griever, that seems counterintuitive. Why, they ask, would you want constant reminders of death? What you and I know is that the grief suit is first and foremost a reminder of the *person* who died, not their death.

What challenges grievers is that they cannot live in a grief suit forever; one must slowly return to life in the present. It can be scary, I know it can, but I have a secret for you—another secret that non-grievers seem not to know: You can put the grief suit, or even just a part of it, back on anytime you want or need to. You see, though grievers cannot live in grief 24/7/365, that does not mean you take off the grief suit never to wear it again. Instead, just like any other article of clothing, you remove it and tuck it away for safe keeping until you need it. Some of you may be asking, "Why would I ever *choose* to wear it?" Well, when the grief waves hit fast and heavy, when special days arrive, when something you were out doing brought your person to mind, when missing them is raw—in those moments, putting on the grief suit can draw you back into your person's presence, comfort you, and give you permission to linger in that place until you are ready to step out of it again.

The grief suit has a purpose, but you also have a purpose. Removing the grief suit allows you the freedom to move and explore and dream as you find the next layer of your identity.

Action Challenge

To remove something, you need to first identify it and the purpose it once served. Apply this to the concept of a grief suit: How does/did yours serve you in the beginning of grief? Has it changed over time? What signals you to put it on or take it off? Explore these questions and anything else that came to mind while reading this Reflection. What promise(s) do you want to make to yourself about your own growth?

TOOLKIT: MY "MORE" LIST

"There is more to learn, more to do, and more people to love."
Faith Doesn't Erase Grief, 36

In considering who you are as you move through changing grief, it can be helpful to brainstorm using the categories of Learn, Do, and Love to describe your new sense of identity. To begin, write whatever comes to mind in each of the three areas. You can sort them later into categories like "What was I thinking?" or "I need to make this happen!" or "Hmmm. Maybe later." For now, start dreaming and play with it without limitations.

Learn:

Do:

Love:

Reflection

"But that doesn't mean your grief will always control your emotions, thoughts, and actions. As you do your grief work, you will learn to control your grief."

Faith Doesn't Erase Grief, 42

Today we turn to a different aspect of identity that is impacted by grief: control over your thoughts, emotions, and actions. Yes, we can learn to control them.

When grief first strikes, a lot of our basic functions stop, well, functioning. People who never needed to rely on lists find themselves creating task lists for everything from paying the bills to moving the laundry over from the washer to the dryer. Some of us might zone out during a routine activity such as driving, to the point that when they come back to awareness, they do not know where they are going. Their brain simply is not working like it did before. It isn't only activities, though; our emotions and thoughts are also impacted. Sometimes grievers find themselves in a pattern of thought that is out of character. For instance, sometimes a griever who never had reactive anger suddenly explodes at the smallest infraction, or someone who was known for their patience becomes exasperated by waiting in a line of only two people. All of this happens outside of their control. That loss of control feels a bit self-betraying, doesn't it? I promise you it does not last. With effort, you can regain that familiar command over your emotions, thoughts, and actions. You will get back what you lost, but you will need to be intentional in your practice to do so.

For example, a person who never needed a list to remember certain tasks before grief now is forgetting everything. They have a choice to make at this juncture. Option A: Get repeatedly frustrated and berate their brain for forgetting everything. Option B: Use a tool to help their memory until the tool is no longer needed. Think of the latter choice as a reclaiming. If you start using a list, your brain will be able to *rest*, which it desperately needs. You can relieve it of the burden of having to remember to empty the dishwasher or schedule the oil change, and this will free up brain space and energy to do the healing work of processing your grief well. In time, your ability to complete tasks on the list without needing to look at it will return. You will regain that control. You can reclaim it.

Action Challenge

Before you move on to whatever is next in your day, write down what came to mind while reading this Reflection. What area of control is most lacking for you right now? Does it primarily involve thought, action, or emotion? What can you do to release your negative reaction to it and begin reclaiming that control by adding practical supports to your life in these areas?

TOOLKIT: THOUGHT CHANGING

The way we view ourselves and our circumstances is almost entirely dictated by the thoughts in our mind, the things we say to ourselves about ourselves or the current situation we're in. *Thought stopping*—reciting phrases or applying techniques that help you stop harmful thoughts—is a wonderful approach but might be too much when you're in the thick of grief. For now, start with *thought changing*: reframing thoughts from negative to positive. It is always a challenging start when I do this in a grief group, but as you try the process and note how different the paired statements feel in your being, I trust you will see the benefit. I started a few for you and encourage you to add your own. I love hearing from my readers, so if you have a statement you cannot seem to change, send it to me through my contact page (see the About the Author); I'm happy to help!

Example 1

Starting point: I'm going to be alone for the rest of my life.

Reframe: I miss my partner and all the ways they filled my life. And I have many other people who also love me. I am not alone; I miss my partner, and that is okay.

Example 2

Starting point: I'll never learn how to do what they did.

Reframe: Right now, I don't know how to do it. I can learn, and I know their friends will help me. If I can't learn or do not want to learn, I can choose to forego it or hire it out. I do not need to do everything they did or how they did it.

Reflection

"Most friendships are seasonal . . . Unfortunately, grief is a time when this comes to light."

Faith Doesn't Erase Grief, 102

Friendships teach us a lot about ourselves because we are drawn to people with whom we resonate in some way. There are friendships that start over a shared love of books, movies, music, or travel; friendships that start through work or mutual friends and then take on a life of their own; and friendships that we have had for so long we cannot recall how they started. Sometimes initial friendships blossom into something deeper, more soul-resonating, but not always. The work friend does not always remain a friend when one of you moves on to a new job, right?

Friendships also change according to continued personal growth, distance, and life influences. Some friendships are meant to be seasonal, and sometimes you meet a person at age thirteen who will be by your side, come what may, until the end of time. When a friendship begins, of course, you do not know what kind of relationship it will ultimately turn into. I would not have made it through college without certain people, but I still have a relationship with only some of them. Unfortunately, it is also when we are fighting through grief that we learn which people in our lives fall into the category of seasonal friends.

The cause of this varies, but know that, for the most part, it has more to do with their discomfort with your grief than anything else. The other piece of the puzzle, though, is that you do change. Think back throughout your life on those friends you thought would be with you forever, but now you do not even exchange birthday texts. If you look closely at possible causes, I am guessing you'll see that at least one of you changed in a significant enough way that the friendship just stopped making sense. There is no blame or fault; it just happened.

Sometimes it's hard to identify what caused the end of the friendship, and sometimes you know you have stepped away because something now feels off. Regardless, the friendship has come to an end, and because you are already grieving, this added loss might feel like a betrayal or abandonment.

I challenge you to try to look at it honestly. It might feel like betrayal, but it might just be the end of a friendship that has served its purpose. For both of you. It is okay to walk away from friendships in grief, and it is okay to feel sad about those who walk away from you. Yes, the people you call friends can tell you a lot about yourself, but they do not define you. The end of a friendship, no matter who instigates it, also does not define you. Give the ending the attention you feel it deserves (which might be none!), and then shift your energy to opening yourself up to new friendships.

Action Challenge

This is a pick-your-own-adventure style challenge. Option 1: Reflect on a friendship that consumes your energy and consider if it is energy well spent. Does the friendship still fit who you are now? Give yourself permission to take whatever next steps you need, whether to say goodbye or to find a way to be open with them about how you feel. Option 2: Set a date to go somewhere that increases the likelihood of meeting new acquaintances who have the potential to become friends.

TOOLKIT: MANTRA BREATHING

Deep breathing, especially when combined with a mantra or repeated word, is a tool commonly used to bring the body a sense of calm and control. You can use deep breathing in moments when people project onto you their thoughts, beliefs, timelines, pain, or anything else that might cause you to lose your sense of who or where you are. For instance, if a person says something that causes you to question if your grief is appropriate, and you do not have the energy to interject or challenge them, use mantra breathing to quickly and easily center yourself back in what you know is true. And, as a bonus, you can do it without them having any idea!

To engage this practice, get in a comfortable position and inhale deeply and slowly through your nose. Hold that breath for a moment before you forcefully, but slowly, exhale through your mouth. Repeat as needed. Using one of the following prepared mantras, or adding one of your own, pace the words to the inhale, hold, and exhale as it feels right to you. Be fluid with this exercise; continue to breathe deeply as you repeat a mantra in your mind. Continue until you feel your tension leave or reduce to a more comfortable level.

I am working my grief at my pace, and I do not need to receive the pressure others place on me.

I am allowed to feel joy and do not need to justify it.

I am allowed to say no without explaining my choice.

I am allowed to honor myself and my own needs.

I am allowed to put my grief away. I will come back to it later.

I am able to sit in my grief when I need to. I have people in my life who will help me know when I've sat too long in it.

Reflection

> "People tend to experience the greatest relief in their changed mood and the return of pleasant emotions."
>
> *Faith Doesn't Erase Grief*, 140

Unpleasant emotions are a particularly uncomfortable thing to have to endure in an already difficult season of life. They feel icky—yes, that's a technical term—under your skin, within the confines of your body.

You know how they say your bedroom should be your sanctuary? The place where you can truly relax and be fully yourself, the place that can transport you to peace? The same can be said of your body. If there's one place we should always feel safe and comfortable, it is in our own body; but in grief, thanks to intense, uncommon, and unpleasant emotions, that often just isn't the case. This is not the worst part of grief, but it certainly does add insult to injury.

And then, one day, something starts to change. Finally, genuinely and without forcing it, you enjoy an activity or laugh at something not at all connected to the person who died. You just see something funny and laugh, naturally! In that moment, you realize you are coming back to yourself. Your returned ability to feel pleasant emotions as they naturally occur has positively changed the way you feel in your own skin. At last, you are once again comfortable, safe, and at home in your own body.

This does not mean the unpleasant emotions are gone, never to return; that's just not a realistic expectation. Life is full of ups and downs, and fluctuating emotions flow out of this, but when you can trust that your default mood and view of the world has returned, there enters a simultaneous trust that you can keep going. You are coming home to yourself.

Action Challenge

Take the temperature of how comfortable you are in your own skin. Did you already go through the thick of it, and now you feel settled in your body, ready to continue moving forward? Or do you feel like a stranger in your own body? Somewhere in the middle? Whatever it is, write the date and a word or phrase to indicate where you are. Then set a reminder on your calendar to return to this page every few weeks or months and reassess. Remember, we're not talking about feeling "better" or "done." This is simply about being comfortable within yourself while you continue the work of grief.

TOOLKIT: TRAJECTORY TRACKER 3

This tool reflects the fact that grief is not steady, linear, predictable, or unidirectional. Here the adage of "one step forward, two steps back" does not apply, though it might feel like it does. The Trajectory Tracker is here to help you in this confusing reality to visualize where you are and where you want to be. Be sure to date a trajectory when you complete it so you can later compare it to others. Hopefully in this way, over time, you will clearly see that you have moved forward overall. If you compare the completed trackers and find that you have *not* moved forward, consider that an indicator you should reach out for more help.

On the next page you will see an image of a path with three main areas: Start, Middle, and Beyond. *Start* indicates the place or time when your thoughts and actions are stuck in the past, with minimal participation in the present and no thoughts of the future. *Middle* signals a shift to a state where you are living more in the present, able both to remember the past without getting caught up in it and to envision the future. *Beyond* is the final stage of the path where you now fully participate in daily life and actively work on building toward the future. You have learned how to carry your loved one's presence with you as you desire and to control when to reflect and remember.

Considering those three main areas, reflect on where you are in the present moment. Are you close to the start, firmly in the middle, or somewhere between? Place a mark along the pathway, indicating the date, to show where you think you are at this point, and add a few comments or sentences about why you placed yourself there. Then write a goal for where you want to be when you complete the next tracker.

Identity 159

Date:

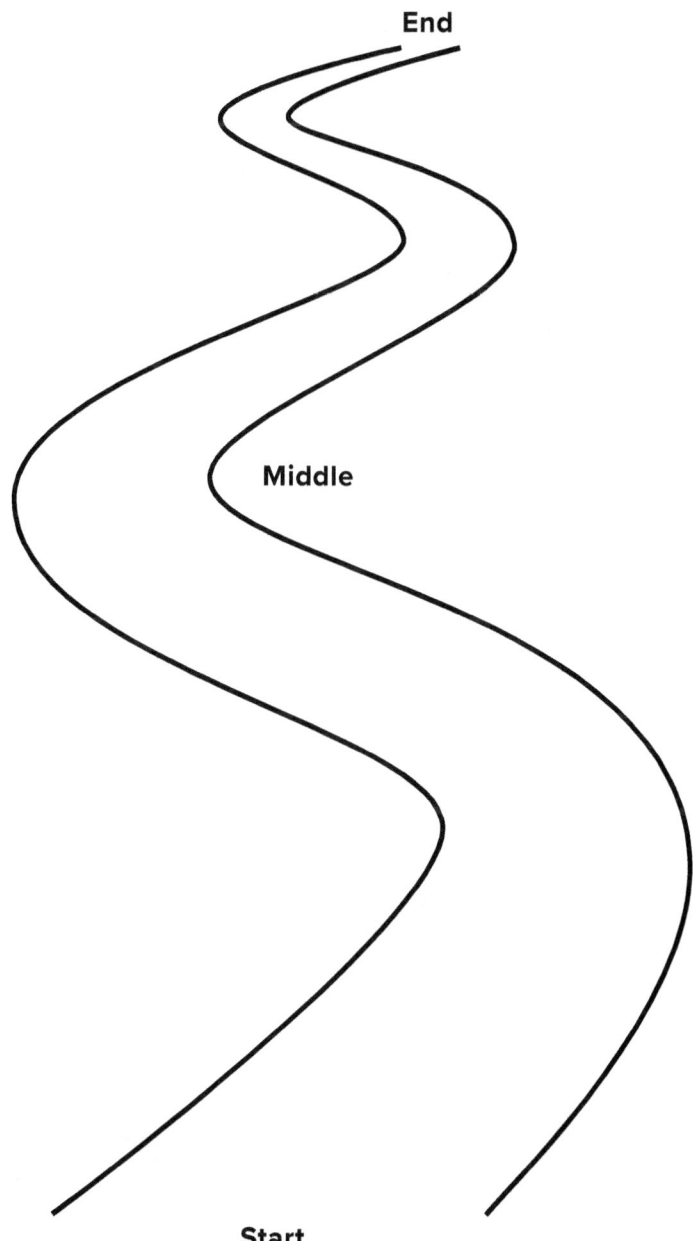

Through

The first three sections of this guidebook—Emotions, Connection, and Identity—shared a common goal of providing you, the griever, with tools to keep you moving amid grief waves. This final section—Through—has a slightly different purpose. In *Faith Doesn't Erase Grief*, I wrote about "finding your through": that thing that keeps you moving rather than avoiding your grief or getting stuck in it. This section builds upon that concept.

Through is about adapting to and integrating the death and your grief into your sense of self so that you can reengage in life unhindered, in a way that is healthy and, to whatever degree you desire, in a way that includes the deceased. To accomplish this, the focus of this section is divided between *handling* the overall grief trajectory—being thrown into Early Grief, persevering through Middle Grief, and enduring Lasting Grief—and *preparing* yourself to deal with the random occurrences of grief waves.

Some Toolkit and Reflection pages in this section will pull together concepts learned in Emotions, Connection, and Identity to more deeply root within you what you've learned about how grief works. Other Toolkits and Reflections will teach you how to take an offensive approach by harnessing control over grief waves to help you anticipate and avoid situations that pose a threat to forward movement. Additionally, this section will give you practice getting unstuck from persistent traps. Here we are going to utilize a lot of self-talk and self-reflection, so consider your capacity for both before you start working in this section. It would be best to complete these pages when you have the space to be still and calm, when you are generally comfortable within yourself.

Through work is necessary for the first whole year after a death, but it is not limited to that timeframe. If you are beyond the first year and something within you drew you to pick up this guidebook, then a piece of you recognizes you are stuck somewhere in your grief. In that case, it might be beneficial to incorporate pages from this section from the beginning of your journey in this book. Regardless of how you apply it, this concept of safe harbor should help pull everything together for you, training you on how to find and feel the hope that will sustain you throughout your grief work.

TOOLKIT: OBJECT LESSON

If you had to illustrate your grief, what would it look like? The image that most resonates with me is that of a large internal ball with sharp edges that poke and prod, inflicting pain from head to toe when I move. Then, as I work at it, it slowly shrinks in size, and the spikes fall off. Draw what your grief looks like and how you carry it in your body. Is it all-consuming? Maybe it's on the smaller side, so that it bounces around your body? Are its edges, sharp, dull, or some of each? Is it small enough that you can keep it in one place, tucked away where it causes minimal pain? Draw (or describe with words if that's more of your thing) what is true of you and your grief right now, and record the date.

Reflection

"Grief steals living from the survivor."

Faith Doesn't Erase Grief, 7

I once worked with a child who drew grief as a masked burglar, and years later, of all the multitude of grief metaphors in existence, I find this one still resonates the most. When they first showed the drawing to me, I asked questions based on the assumption that the burglar was a representation of death, that the burglar stole the person who had died. That made sense to me, so it was the direction I went, but the artist quickly corrected me. As they started naming items in the burglar's bag, I realized they were instead telling me about the many things stolen from them because of the death.

For this child, the bag carried things like safety, protection, play, sleep, and fun—in technical terms, it carried secondary losses. Many people are unfamiliar with the concept of secondary losses like this. We become so focused on the absence of the person's physical presence that we don't immediately see the domino effect of related losses. The space a person takes up in our life is so much more than their physical presence, and when they die, we are forced to find different ways to receive those same things. The problem is grief creates a barrier that prevents us from seeing how to go about doing that.

To move through grief, we need to be honest with ourselves about the fullness of what was lost. Only in naming everything that has been lost can we determine what can be left behind and what needs to find a new source. Let's say your person fostered in you a sense of confidence. As you move through the depths of grief, how will you find ways to grow your self-confidence? Are there ways to remind yourself of how they did that for you? Is there another person in your sphere who can take on that role?

Finding your way through is not about you or anyone else stepping into the space of the person who died and taking over. Rather, it is about identifying those things that the person helped grow and shape in you and seeking ways to retain them, albeit differently, in your new reality. The Grief Thief only wins when we throw in the towel. You are a created and creative being meant to move through this chapter of life and into the next, not by leaving your person behind but by relocating their position in your life so you can focus on what is in front of you now.

Action Challenge

Write your person a letter thanking them for everything they fostered in you and everything they showed you about yourself. Tell them how you will continue growing and recognizing those traits within yourself. Alternatively, write them a letter expressing your disappointment, anger, frustration, sadness, or whatever emotions you hold for all that is in you that they did *not* recognize or that their actions hindered. Include how you will continue working to develop those pieces of yourself because they will no longer hold you back.

Whichever letter you write, complete a ritual to signify the end of the experience: Tuck it away, bury it, burn it, tear it up, or put it in a journal; whatever you choose, do something that will help you continue moving forward.

TOOLKIT: THE BURGLAR'S BAG

Take some time to reflect, allowing your mind to open and think broadly about what the Grief Thief stole from you. Again, this is not about what the *death* stole from you; this is about what your subsequent grief has taken from you. For example, your confidence, excited anticipation of the future, plans, hopes, safety, security, love, peace, or trust—write whatever comes to you in the illustrated bag. It's extra-large to allow for your freedom of expression. You may draw the items instead or tape representative pictures onto the bag. You can use different colors or writing styles to represent the different levels of impact the items have. Did grief steal something you do not want back? Cover it with the words "thank you" or "goodbye." Have you done enough work to be able to reclaim something that was stolen? Symbolically "remove" it from the bag by detaching the taped item or erasing/covering the word or image and putting it on a sticky note instead, which you can attach to your fridge or bathroom mirror to remind you of what is yours once again.

Through

Reflection

> "It is in feeling these unpleasant emotions that we move forward."
> *Faith Doesn't Erase Grief*, 98

"What if I'm doing something wrong? I mean, I'm worried there is something I'm supposed to be doing that I'm not doing." Clients ask this or similar questions because they are either (a) trying to convince themselves they are doing grief work when they aren't or (b) truly not feeling the work they are doing is sufficient, and my first task when a client poses this question is to determine which category the client is in.

The goal of group A is not to move forward—it is to move on. In other words, they want to do just enough to get by and *appear* fine to the people in their circle. The goal of group B is different. They know, either from experience or from exposure to grief in some other way (such as reading about it or observing others), that moving forward does not happen without first moving *through* the unpleasant, painful, undesirable emotions.

Ask yourself: How are we told to survive quicksand? *Do not fight it.* This sentiment also holds true for moving forward and finding your way through grief. Resisting or avoiding the unpleasant emotions is like flailing your arms in a pit of quicksand; nothing good comes of it, and it only sinks you deeper, faster.

You can avoid getting stuck in the emotional quicksand of grief with honesty. It is just that challenging and just that simple. Without honestly engaging this process, a griever can make a very good show of moving forward, but they will only do so at a surface level. For months, even years, they might play the part of a healing griever by reengaging in life and building relationships so that others are convinced they found their "through." But just under the surface, they have a bundle of repressed emotions looking for escape, and—I guarantee—they *will* find their escape, likely in a far more destructive way than if the griever faced them from the start. This is because the griever has left a piece of themselves stuck in that quicksand, and eventually they will need to return and face what caused that piece to be left behind in the first place.

Here is the hope: It truly is never too late to retrieve what is stuck in the quicksand. Never. If you found your way to this guidebook years after someone's death, I promise you can still do the work to get unstuck. Will it be comfortable? Probably not. But the relief you will feel at finally bringing to light what you have avoided all this time will outweigh the pain. And to finally experience what it is to truly, fully move forward? Better than words can convey.

Action Challenge

Assess your goal for grief work. Would you place yourself in group A, meaning you picked up this book to get on with getting *over* grief? Or do you fit better with group B, meaning you know it is time to start the hard work of grief, and you wanted something to guide you through? What do you want from the time you put into these pages?

Next Level

Identify any pieces of you that are stuck in grief's quicksand and create a plan to connect with a professional who can help you to get unstuck, safely and calmly. Set calendar alerts to hold yourself accountable for taking those steps.

TOOLKIT: PSALM 23

Reading Psalm 23 through a grief lens can change the way in which you view yourself, the process of grief, and even your relationship with God. Using the grief lens of through, read Psalm 23 in a few different translations. For each of the following words, write a short reflection in the space provided on how it informs your grief experience. In what ways might the word change how you grieve? In what ways does it change how you view God? These words are only enough to get you started; if you resonate deeply with other words from the psalm, add them to the page along with your reflections.

Walk

Through

Valley

Rest

Renew

Reflection

> "Try to stop yourself from being drawn into the trap of comparison; nothing good ever comes from it, and it can have a negative impact on your own progress."
>
> *Faith Doesn't Erase Grief*, 37

I can speak with the authority born from experience that middle school wreaks havoc on adolescent girls and their friendships. Between hormone floods (completely out of our control) and nonstop comparisons (completely within our control), all relationships feel like they are on the brink of a disastrous, drama-filled end. Thankfully we grow out of many of these patterns, but regardless of gender, comparison with others is one trap most adults never entirely escape. Grief is no exception.

If the purpose of grief work is to learn to weather grief waves, integrate grief into our lives, and reengage with daily activities, think of comparison as public enemy number one. There is no one else who can tell you precisely how to work through your grief, so comparing your experience and needs directly to someone else's is a moot point. Not a top-rated grief expert, not all the books on all the shelves in all the world, not your pastor, not your best friend—not even someone grieving the same person knows what's best for you. Each of these people can serve a supportive role and point out obstacles or gifts you might otherwise miss; experts and books can provide guidance and a heads-up of what might be in front of you. But only you know what is right to keep you moving forward and through.

My maternal grandma was the epitome of a matriarch. She loved each of us individually as we were, and she loved bringing us all together. She fed us, she played with us, she made us laugh. Myra left an indelible mark on the family system, on each of her siblings, her adoring husband, children, grandchildren, and great-grandchildren. Even the ones she never met benefit from all she embodied and shared. And yet not one of us grieves her in the same way. There are similarities between us, of course, stories we all love to tell and shared experiences we all miss. Even with those similarities, though, my grief work was and is different from that of my mom, who grieves differently than grandma's sister, and on it goes. Why is that? Because despite all the shared elements of grief in my family, *my* relationship with Grandma was unique to the two of us. No one else knows *exactly* what it was.

Action Challenge

A concrete way to avoid comparing and advice giving is to remove "should" from your vocabulary and instead embrace experience sharing. "Shoulds" trap you and others, but experiencing sharing helps us move through the trap into active living.

To get you started, try phrases like "When I feel like that, it helps me to [fill in the blank]. Maybe that will help you too?" or "The first annual marker for me was tough, and I wish I had accepted the offers of help from friends. If you want to know more about that, let me know." Take some of the advice you received from other people or found in books that proved helpful for you and rewrite it into experience you can share with others. Ask them to adopt the same approach with you. The more you all practice this new phrasing, the better you will avoid comparing grief with one another, which will result in more enjoyable and beneficial conversations.

TOOLKIT: MAP IT OUT

"Moving forward is about choosing what parts of the past come with you and what changes you want to make, all while carrying the memory of your loved one as you see fit."
Faith Doesn't Erase Grief, 43

Finding your grief through line is not a one-time decision or a simple act of willpower. It takes thought, intention, experimentation, and a whole lot of self-grace. With that in mind, use the following open space to illustrate how you might personally apply the opening definition of moving forward. To my fellow non artists: Instead of drawing the parts of the past that come with you and those that don't, you can log them solely with words. The point is to consider if and how you want the person who died to come along with you. What parts from your past life need to remain in the past, and what do you want to join you in the future? Give your creative brain some time to play. I encourage you to use one color (or set of colors) for this first round, whether you're writing or drawing, and date the results; then in a few months or even a year or more down the road, revisit this page and add to your list or create a new illustration to match your reality at that time.

Reflection

> "Each of them learned that though the person's death would forever impact them, that day did not need to define the remainder of their lives."
>
> *Faith Doesn't Erase Grief*, 144

We talk often of moments in life that are *defining*, but have you ever thought about the weight of that word? Giving a single moment the power to define one's life can throw a lot out of balance, and grief is no different. If you allow a death in your life the power to be wholly definitive, then grief wins.

Life is filled with turning points: departure lines to unexpected routes, unanticipated ups and downs. Each of these moments tend to result in things like self-reflection, reconsideration, reconciliation, and maybe even forgiveness, but they do not need to rise to the level of completely defining. The difference here is in the onus of control.

Events that happen outside of our control, such as death, leave us reeling. In the aftermath, though, we get to choose what those events mean for the rest of our lives. *You* are the one who decides if death has the power to define your life, thrusting upon you a new label that can never be removed. But if you decide that whatever happened does not get to define you, even if it impacts you enormously, then you also get to choose when the label of that event applies to you and when it doesn't.

At the start of my time working with the family referenced in the opening quote, they had taken on a number of labels given to them by their faith community, their school community, their extended family, and even their own minds: Failure. Disappointment. Bad parent. Ignorant. Blind. At every turn, they were met with judgment and blame and could not see a way forward. During the course of our work together, each person unpacked their own pieces of trauma and guilt and anger, and as a family system, they fought through a perceived need to stay frozen in time so that they could continue living without guilt for moving forward. In other words, they learned how to choose when the label of "griever" no longer felt right as the primary label for each individual or for the family as a whole.

Their loved one's death will forever impact them, without a doubt. Their person's imprint is lasting, and they will feel the absence at every future family event and significant moments. And yet, individually and as a family, they came to understand that they had a lot of life left to explore. To continue using "griever" as their primary title would only hold them back from living. Similarly, finding your way through grief will be in part dependent on learning the difference between being impacted by something and being defined by it. Impact is inevitable, but definition is a choice.

Action Challenge

In what ways have you allowed this death to define you? Are you holding on to the label of "griever" for longer than you need? If you are, consider why that is. What do you fear will happen if that label is moved to the bottom of the list? Take a few moments to determine if you are impacted or defined by your person's death; then, if needed, start taking steps to free yourself enough to resume moving forward. Review what you've already completed in the Identity section and choose a piece of identity you can focus on, such as resuming a hobby, going back to work, returning to a family role you've put to the side since the death. You do not need to go straight from A to Z, but take small, consistent steps at a pace that is comfortable.

TOOLKIT: GUIDED FREE ASSOCIATION

As mentioned in several places in this workbook, Guided Free Association is a tool to help clients uncover those things that need to come to the surface in order to move beyond them. In this section, the focus of the exercise is *through*. Where in grief are you stuck? Is there a way through that you simultaneously long for and fear? How do you envision getting through? This tool will assist you in answering these and similar questions to help you break free from what is holding you back. Read through all the steps *before* beginning so you are prepared to move seamlessly through the process.

Step 1: Choose a Focus Word related to finding your way through. If you feel stuck at some point in your grief, using "stuck" as a word could be your first step. Maybe you feel ready to invest in the future but don't know where to begin; in that case, "dream" or "hope" could be good Focus Words. Perhaps using the word "through" itself could reveal a lot. Choose your word and write it here:

Step 2: Start a timer for fifteen to thirty seconds and stare at your Focus Word, repeating it in your mind until the timer sounds.

Step 3: Start a timer for ten to fifteen minutes and begin writing. Let your intuition take over and allow your words to meander wherever they want to go. Have another sheet of paper or a laptop nearby in case you need more room.

Step 4: When the timer sounds, stop writing. Move from the space where you completed this activity and do something soothing and preferably physical. Take a shower, go for a walk, call a friend. If you want to process what you wrote, I encourage you to do so with a therapist or trusted friend.

Through

Reflection

> "Each step forward is a step closer to healing. Healing, remember, is not about removing the grief but about accommodating and eventually befriending it to gain control over it."
>
> Faith Doesn't Erase Grief, 96

I'd been working with one client for several months and, if I'm being honest, was discouraged at what appeared to be a lack of forward movement. Because of the level of trauma tied to her spouse's death, she struggled to move past the intrusive thoughts and images from the day it happened, which in turn increased the difficulty of reengaging in the rest of life. She did manage to pay her bills, feed her animals, and keep her house and herself clean—all major victories in grief. Yet on another level she was completely stuck, afraid to move through her trauma.

"Why can't I get over this? I do not want to feel like this all the time!" Those words were the crack in the door I had been waiting for. We talked about what moving forward looked like to her and what her fears were about it, and she was finally able to tell me that even though it was almost unbearably painful, holding on to that day allowed her to feel connected to her spouse. *Ah, I remember thinking, that is the key. She needs to know he is not going anywhere if she moves beyond the day of his death.*

Through a lot of talk and creative expression, honest reflection, and opening herself to possible other ways to connect with her spouse, she was finally able to push beyond the day of death and shed the trauma. "I feel lighter. I can walk through my house without anxiety, and I can even drive past places that meant a lot to us and experience the good memories. There's still pain, and I'm sure there always will be at least some pain, but now I get the good parts of our story too."

This client took control of her grief by working directly with what she most feared, and in doing that, she learned that she had the power to decide what healing means to her. She could decide the role grief would and would not play as she stepped back into wholehearted living. She could be fully present with her children and grandchildren again, fully present at work, and fully present when she accepted invitations to spend time with others.

This is what it means to accommodate and befriend grief, to integrate it into continued living instead of focusing on that one certain day in the past. The person who died is so much more than their death, and your connection to them goes on beyond that day too.

Action Challenge

Where are you stuck? What are you afraid to release to move forward? Be honest with yourself about your fears. Then, when you are ready, allow your creative mind to enact a ritual of release: Envision yourself taking the first step toward healing. How will it feel in your body to no longer be trapped in that place? Know that it is not a betrayal of the person who died to not remain stuck in grief. Trust that you will find new, healthier, and more comforting ways to connect with them if you so desire.

TOOLKIT: HORIZON LINE

"The road of grief is often like hiking in a sand dune. It is long and challenging with no indication of relief. But as you near the water, you feel a breeze, and you come over the final hill to something unexpected and beautiful. The horizon greets you with a promise of *continued life*, renewed purpose, and the *hope that you will carry your loved one with you into your next adventure*."

Faith Doesn't Erase Grief, 41, emphasis added

This Toolkit activity is found in the last three sections of this book, each with a slightly different emphasis depending on the theme of that section. Today, consider what your horizon might look like as it relates to the next chapter in your life. What is in the foreground? What awaits you in the distance? What is the promise beyond the horizon? If you connect with the sand dune image in the opening quote, ask yourself if you're still climbing the dune or cresting it with a close view of the water. Do you prefer a desert scene? Perhaps a cityscape? Reread the opening quote, listen to what stirs in your heart and mind, and draw an image of that below. If drawing intimidates you, that's okay! Use colors or words around the provided horizon line to create an image in your mind in whatever way works for you.

Reflection

> "You do not need to rush through to the other side, and moving forward and continuing to live does not mean letting go of your person."
>
> *Faith Doesn't Erase Grief,* 194

"I'm never going to be ready to leave this group." I usually heard this statement from participants after the first three sessions of a spousal loss support group I facilitated. Entering the group and being met with validation, support, encouragement, and hope is a powerful enough experience to make a person's shoulders release tension and their lungs exhale a deep breath. It is such a different feeling than what is experienced *outside* of the group that the idea of one day also losing this connection is too much to bear.

There are two seemingly opposing root causes for this worry: Participants believe they need to finish their grief work on a set timetable, but they also believe that if they stop actively working on their grief, they will let go of and possibly forget their person. These are both false worries, I promise! I've listed here three reasons I *know* you can use to release this worry, and I trust you will find in them a sense of peace, hope, and reassurance.

1. Grief is not a race. A race implies a finish line, which grief does not have. It gets better, shifts, changes, and lessens, but there isn't any line that you need to cross in a set timeframe. No one is allowed to rush you through your grief, not even you.
2. When the day comes—and it will—that your grief is not the dominant thought in your mind and heart, you can reassure yourself that you've not left your person behind but instead relocated them to a safe, protected, easily accessible space.

3. You cannot forget your person. Whether you have known them for years or never had the chance to meet them in this world, what you know of them remains. You impacted their life, and they impacted yours, and those imprints are not going anywhere.

Action Challenge

Create something you can turn to as needed, no matter how many days, weeks, months, or years go by, and be reminded that your connection is always accessible. Put together a photo collage; create an alphabetical list with one trait or memory of the person and/or your relationship for each letter; start a list of the first five to ten things that come to mind about your person, and then add to it whenever something new comes to mind. Then, whenever you use what you create, pay attention to how quickly the memories rush back, how closely you feel their presence, and the balance of gratitude, sadness, and joy as you remember.

TOOLKIT: VICTORY WALL

As a counselor, I open each support group session or individual session I facilitate with a time to share victories, no matter how small they might appear, because recognizing victories is one way that finding our way through happens. When the brain or heart tries to convince us we're stuck, we can look to our victories as proof that movement is in fact happening.

Today, I want you to start your own victory wall by drawing squares in the space that follows: These will represent plaques or certificates commemorating your personal victories. Mark the page and come back to enter victories as they occur. Alternatively, start a literal victory wall in your home with sticky notes, chalkboard paint, or a giant dry-erase board. Make whatever it is easily visible so you don't lose sight of progress. Also, when I say no matter how small, I do mean every little thing. The first time you buy groceries only for yourself. The first time you make a large purchase on your own. The first time you go alone to a movie your person would love. The first day you notice a little less pain at the thought or sound of their name. The first time you take a trip. It all counts. And yes, repeated activities count too! You get to decide what is a victory—just be generous with yourself and write them all down so you have the encouragement when you need it.

My Victory Wall

Reflection

"Try."

Faith Doesn't Erase Grief, 20

You know the saying "the only way out (or over something) is through"? While I do not like the notion of something being entirely "over," because we are always impacted by our losses, the *through* part is spot-on. Once you accept that denying, avoiding, or stuffing grief will only serve to delay the release of its current weight, you can begin shedding that weight one action at a time. That doesn't mean focusing on forward movement isn't challenging for grievers; working through intense emotions and slogging through the early days requires a lot of us, which means having the desire, let alone the capacity, to reengage in the rest of life can feel unimaginable. I will not deny that it is difficult—of course it is. The world you knew is no longer, and somehow you are expected to continue as if that is not the case.

Impossible as it may seem, you can do this. I promise, you can. I can't tell you your starting point, but I can give you the how. Ready? *Try*. Yes, it is that simple. Try. The world you knew and loved and trusted changed, but to find your way through, you *can* work to enter this new world, to put it together in a way that restores familiarity and safety and love and hope. I know that sounds like a tall order, but as with the entire grief process, it is something you do one piece at a time.

Let's walk through an example together. Let's say there is a restaurant you two frequented that you've not gone to since they died. First, decide whether or not you want to go back. In other words, did you go to that restaurant because it made them happy, or do you also enjoy it? If you did not enjoy it, scrap it; you are not obligated to go back there. If you do enjoy the food, then move forward through the "Try Plan." As a first step, have the food delivered or pick it up curbside. If it is enough for you to enjoy the food again, you can pause there. But maybe when you taste the food again, you realize the atmosphere of the restaurant is just as important. For your next step, try to return, either by yourself or with someone who will give you the space to work through your process. Experiment with it. See what works and what doesn't. The point, the only point, is to try.

Most importantly, if the attempt does not go well, try again another time, unless you realized in the attempt that it truly isn't that important. If it did not go well at first, you just weren't ready, and that's okay. You will only know when you are ready if you try.

Action Challenge

Create a Try Plan for the activity or place that came to mind when you read today's Reflection. Break it down into small pieces with as much detail as possible. Will you do this solo or with others? Is there a specific person who would be helpful to take with you? Consider *why* this particular thing is important to you, and keep that reason in mind each time you try. Remember, go slow. For today, simply write out the Try Plan. That's it. You are not starting the process today; save that for later (but set a date for step one!). You can do this!

TOOLKIT: CLAIMING OWNERSHIP

"Moving forward is a statement of ownership over grief, not a removal of it."

Faith Doesn't Erase Grief, 191

When you land in Lasting Grief, a phase marked by consistently moving forward, you have found your way through. One signpost that you have made it is the transition from passive grief to active grief. In other words, you have now taken ownership and can tell grief when it is time for a break or a pause. You are able to tell grief that it is no longer allowed to dominate your being. I know this is difficult to imagine, but grief will come to listen.

Will grief waves still arrive without warning? Yes. In those situations, control will manifest in your ability to not be derailed for a week by the wave or even for a full day. Believe me, seizing that ownership is empowering!

As you look forward to this, write a message to grief. What do you want to say to it? What does it need to know for you to make peace with its existence (in other words, to befriend it)? This is a moment of ownership that I hope you take—empower yourself. You can do this!

Reflection

> "Moving forward, not moving on: that is the goal of grief work. Forward versus on."
>
> *Faith Doesn't Erase Grief*, 42

Every single client, and I mean *every one*, asks this question at some point in the counseling process: "How do you listen to this all day, every day?" Typically, a client poses this question just before they leave, completely depleted, at the end of a challenging or highly emotional session, especially if they are aware I likely have another session (or three) ahead of me. I look forward to the question not only because having the capacity to think outside of themselves signals forward movement in their process, but also because of the answer I get to give them. The answer is this: No matter where a griever begins their grief work, there is always a turning point, a shift, when light returns to their eyes and conversation during sessions is more present tense than past tense. A moment when, unprompted, they share the ways they recognize progress. In short, the moment when hope returns.

The difference between moving forward and moving on is slight, so slight that most people cannot see it until they are in the thick of grief. "Moving on" might sound good, but it carries with it a connotation of somehow finishing grief completely. It's as if there is a point at which a griever will walk out of the front door and say, "Okay, I am ready to proceed with life as if nothing happened and nothing changed." No. That doesn't happen. Now, there is a strong possibility that you have Team Moving On people in your life. You'll recognize them when they change a conversation away from the person who died, pressure you into their timetable, or ask things like "Why are you still sad?" Everything they do, intentionally or not, tells grievers they need to hurry up and finish their grief. Know that it is okay to remove yourself from those relationships or conversations.

Team Moving Forward people, in contrast, follow your lead for the pace you take. They are comfortable with your range of emotions, and they celebrate each of your forward steps no matter how big or small. They support you as you build your new world and help you to keep your person in that world to the degree that you want.

Do you feel the difference? Forward acknowledges the ways you and your world have changed. Forward motivates you to keep moving through the challenges, to face the waves. Forward creates space for pauses and breaks and rest. Forward is what returns light to your eyes and ushers in hope. Release the pressure you feel to move *on*; instead, embrace the processes you can do to move *forward*.

Action Challenge

Choose one of these two questions to answer: How will you know you are moving forward in your grief? Who are the Team Moving Forward people in your life, and how can you allow them to support you?

TOOLKIT: MOVING FORWARD

There is a moment in grief when the griever regains the ability to focus on the present and dream about the future, and that is what moving forward is all about. To that end, this Toolkit is all about dreaming. What do you want life to look like in the future? What in that image is different than your life right now, and how can you get from here to there? Use the rest of this page to describe or draw your dream(s) for the future. You can limit your dreaming to one specific area of life, such as your job, where to live, or how you spend your free time, or you can divide the page into sections and dream about multiple areas. There is no wrong answer, and there are no limits. If you need it, consider this your reminder that to dream is not to betray or forget the one who died. To dream honors the fact that you need to continue living and do so in a way that might look different without them. So, dream. Dream big and dream bold.

Reflection

"We grieve because we love, and loving others is the DNA God implanted in us. To avoid relationships out of fear is to deprive the self of connection, which is one of the most basic needs we have."

Faith Doesn't Erase Grief, 193

Depending on how you're working your way through this guidebook, this might feel like a bit of déjà vu, and in a sense you are correct. I use this same quote elsewhere; however, the lens has changed. The other Reflection with this quote addresses it through the connection lens, but here we consider it via the through lens.

The ability to stay in the present and dream about the future is a trademark of through, and this includes opening yourself to new relationships as they present themselves. If you are grieving a spouse, hear me: Through does *not* need to include a new romantic relationship. It's okay if it does, and for those who desire it, those relationships can be even better than hoped. A griever can, though, reach the phase of through and embrace the remaining chapters of life without ever entering a new romantic relationship.

Remember, through is about continuing to live, and because of the love DNA implanted within us, continuing to live does involve remaining open to the continued development of existing relationships and the possibility of new relationships, whether platonic or romantic. In short, if you want to know you've reached the through phase, look at how you engage your own life as well as how you pour into and receive from other people.

As with all pieces of grief work, this is not something you need to arrive at all at once. Start slowly. Maybe you could be the one to initiate contact this week with the person or people who were steadily by your side these last months. Invite a small group of people to your home for a low-key meal, or even just snacks on the patio. Ask someone to join you at a movie you want to see. Go by yourself to a class of any kind (exercise, art, cooking, etc.) and strike up a conversation with one or two other participants. Love flows naturally through you. Allow it to do so, and it will help you return to fully living.

Action Challenge

Using those suggestions, gently step outside of your comfort zone sometime in the next seven days. Reflect on how it feels to again be able to invest in someone else's life rather than only receiving. Remember, this is a process, so give yourself permission to go slowly (while still moving!).

TOOLKIT: DEMYSTIFYING THE DARK VALLEY

We talk about the power of Psalm 23 in this guidebook, but its "dark valley" can be intimidating, especially when you are more familiar with the language of "shadow of the valley of death." I don't think darkness needs to be scary, though; I think we can change our relationship with it. The goal is not to change what it is or to minimize its impact; rather, the goal is to turn on the light. Turning on the light removes the dark valley's paralyzing power and reminds you that you *can* find your way through the darkness.

To begin, create an image of how you imagine the dark valley. Draw one yourself on the following page or find pictures to tape onto the page. After you've done this, add features that take away the intimidating aspects of the darkness. Have fun with this! What light source(s) do you want? What is on the ground that makes you smile? What is guiding you from the sky? Channel your inner child, and convert the dark valley into something silly.

Mark this page and come back to it whenever you feel the dark valley taking over. Eventually your brain will automatically bring the new image to mind each time you think of the valley. It won't erase the darkness, but it will help remove the fear and make it all a bit easier to navigate.

Reflection

"Lasting grief is maybe best described as a 'settling in,' a time of learning how to get comfortable and adjust to changes, how to build your life around your grief, rather than letting your life be guided by grief."

Faith Doesn't Erase Grief, 139

The house was now hers alone, and in most areas of the home, she was adapting, but the room that housed his prized collection, where he had spent so much time, was an exception. It was too stark a reminder of his absence, so she kept the door closed; the idea of facing the sights, memories, scents, and sounds so closely associated with him was more than she could bear. And yet, she wanted to.

Over the course of the first few months this client met with me, she worked to make the room a neutral space she could pass by without losing her breath, even when the door was open. From there it developed into a place in which she could connect with him. As life around her returned to "normal," the room became a place that allowed her to visit with him, free of any judgment or rushing. It stayed that way for months, and she welcomed it.

And then she turned an unexpected corner. "It's time." She said this one day before even taking her seat in my office. When I asked for more context, suspecting what she meant but needing confirmation, she repeated, "It's time. I want that space! I have worked so hard to get comfortable in the house and make it mine, and that room is just in the way. I love him and I know that room meant a lot to him, but I need it to change. I know I won't lose more of him if I change it. So, I'm changing it."

She'd found her through. She spent the remainder of our session sharing her intentions for his collection (what she would keep, give to important people, or donate) and her thoughts on reclaiming and repurposing the room. She had reached the understanding that making these changes was not a betrayal of her spouse, nor did it signal a lack of love or grief; it simply meant she was ready to fully live. For this woman, dealing with her husband's collection and changing that room was an outward sign to herself that she had learned how to relocate the grief to a place easily accessed yet less prominent in her life.

That is what I mean by through, that is, building a life that includes grief but doesn't focus on it, and this cannot be done on anyone's timetable but your own. If you continue working with your grief, you *will* get there. I have no doubt. Keep at it. Your through is waiting for you.

Action Challenge

What is the equivalent in your grief story to the collector's room? What is the next step you can take toward finding your through? Maybe you're at the beginning and need to reach a neutral position on whatever's holding you back. Maybe you've accepted its presence and are beginning to experience it as a safe place to connect with your person. Maybe you're halfway between it being a place of connection and a place you are ready to reclaim. Without pressuring yourself to take the next step, write out what you anticipate your next few steps will be. Sometimes exposing yourself to the possibilities removes the fear of the unknown and allows you to more easily embrace the future.

TOOLKIT: WANT/NEED ASSESSMENT

"A piece of embracing life is learning—again or for the first time—to think about your own wants and needs."

Faith Doesn't Erase Grief, 185

In support groups, honoring your own needs is by far one of the most challenging assignments for participants to complete. It is so ingrained in many of us to think only about the wants and needs of others that we struggle to recognize, let alone voice, our own desires. To find your through and move forward in life, however, you need to know what it is you need and want in life. Following are a few sentence starters for you to complete with the first thing that comes to mind. Once you've done this, use the remainder of the space to keep going with whatever occurs to you next. In private practice I call this Life Mapping. Use what you write to guide the creation of your next chapter; what you long for will likely bring you contentment, a sure sign you are where God desires you to be.

If I could design the perfect home, it would . . .

If I could spend my days however I wanted, I would . . .

If I could do whatever I wanted for work, I would . . .

I choose to spend my time . . .

The people closest to me . . .

I long for . . .

I can't wait to . . .

Reflection

> "On day 366 after your loved one's death, it is as if people in your life expect you to come out of your house shouting, 'Ta-da! I'm all better now!'"
>
> *Faith Doesn't Erase Grief*, 152

As indicated in the opening quote, those unfamiliar with grief continue to hold an expectation that grievers need only a year to "get better," that somehow living a year without the deceased is sufficient time to remove all signs of grief and pain. With that expectation comes a related belief that on day 366 grievers will return to who they were. Grievers know that is not true, though the pressure surrounding days 365 and 366 remains. The list of statements that follows helps you advocate for yourself and manage your expectations for both day 365 and day 366, whether those days are right around the corner, months away, or in the rearview mirror.

1. Day 365 is not a magical day that will end your grief because in many ways grief does not end. It changes, but it doesn't end.
2. You do not need to relive or reexperience the death on day 365. You are safe and do not need to endure that experience again. You will remember it, of course, but it does not need to be the sole experience of the day. As that day approaches, if you notice your body begin to tense or feel otherwise out of sorts, consciously remind yourself that you are safe and you never need to live through that death again. Your brain will then send that signal of safety to your body, allowing it to relax.
3. You get to choose how much *or how little* attention you give to day 365. You can choose to call it a marker rather than an anniversary, and you also get to choose what you do—or do not do—on that day.

4. Day 365 is an opportunity to remember the fullness of the person's life, not their death. Honor their imprint on your life and the lives of everyone who knew them.
5. Day 365 is *also* an opportunity to acknowledge and maybe even celebrate the work you've done and how far you've come since day one. Do not skip this piece.
6. Day 366 is not a signal that you must move on and forget about grief. Remember, the goal is not to "get over" your grief, but to adapt to and integrate the changes that followed the person's death into how you now live. The effort this takes does not disappear simply because you finished the first year.
7. Day 366 is symbolic of all the days to come in which the absence of your loved one's physical presence is abundant. Birthdays, graduations, anniversaries, weddings, and less obvious days that only you might experience will continue to roll through. On those days, grief waves are likely to return because no matter if it is day 366 or day 1,527, that person is still not physically present.
8. Day 366 does not need to be the start of "the hardest year." Many grievers report being told to watch out for year two because it is "so much worse." But you've done your work. You know how to cope with grief waves, and your expectations are realistic. You have set yourself to keep moving forward. Let the rest unfold one day at a time; don't borrow trouble.

I hope in that list you find the empowerment and encouragement to approach these two days with a clear sense of control, power, and choice instead of passively waiting for something horrible to happen. Remember, you hold the power to make these days whatever you want and need them to be.

Action Challenge

If day 365 and day 366 are still in front of you, start a list of ideas for how you can handle each of those days. On the one-year mark, how might you acknowledge, honor, and remember the fullness of the life lived and relationship shared? How can you set up day 366 to center on how you are heading into the present and future—not leaving the past behind, but tucking it safely away for you to access when needed?

If you are beyond the first year of grief, start a list of ideas for how you might honor the presence of your person on all the significant days and special occasions still to come.

Reflection

> "Remember that moving forward is about returning to living; it is about resuming the process of seeking to become a more complete picture of who God created you to be."
> *Faith Doesn't Erase Grief*, 190

> *"Still, God, you are our Father. We're the clay and you're our potter: All of us are what you made us."*
> Isaiah 64:8, MSG

"You are the potter; I am the clay" is one of those catchphrases many Christians use but don't often stop to consider. Throughout this guide you've encountered reminders that grief changes a person's entire being; so, then, how do we reconcile the idea of God as potter when our whole being has changed? In other words, is God the source of the changes you experience in grief?

To understand the idea of God as the potter of your life, it is helpful to begin by releasing, at least temporarily, any notions you have of God as all-knowing and all-powerful. Shift your starting point of relating to God to this instead: "God's love for you is intimate, unconditional, inescapable, and abiding" (*Faith Doesn't Erase Grief*, 194).

If the starting point to understanding God as potter is God's vast love rather than God's knowledge or power, the image and impact of God as potter flows more easily. I am a created being; therefore, God knows me intimately. Because God knows me intimately, God is fully aware of the enduring changes resulting from my grief. God's love and acceptance of me is unconditional, and therefore regardless of these changes and how they change (or do not change) the direction I take in life, God's love comes with me. My changes cannot prevent God's presence and love from breaking through to me. God loves me abidingly. Through the highs and lows of life, of faith, of questions and doubt, God's love abides. Through even the hardest changes that feel enormous and life-altering, God's love abides.

If all of that is true, then God as potter means that God continues to alter the clay as the needs of the vessel change, right? We each have a purpose as created beings, and through my encounters with the dying and with the grieving, my concept of "purpose" has expanded. Just as a single vessel can serve a variety of purposes, so the purpose of each created being cannot be limited to one label. Reflecting God's light and love to all we meet is the primary, foundational purpose of every created being (and of all of nature, I'd argue), but that's not your *sole* purpose. As you change through seasons of grief, the potter is right there shifting, shaving, adding, and molding to prepare you for whatever you need.

Action Challenge

What went through your heart and mind as you read this Reflection? Did you resist it? Find hope in it? Did it cause you worry or discomfort? Did a part of you long for it to be true? Whatever you experienced, write to God about it. As with everything else I've written, I don't want you to simply take my word for all this: Explore it with God. Now is the time, because you found your through. It is time for you to embark upon your next chapter—and remember, however you choose to take your person with you, that is how it should be. Regardless of what that looks like for you, know you are never alone. The Spirit is right there with you to help you adjust as needed.

TOOLKIT: TRAJECTORY TRACKER 4

This tool reflects the fact that grief is not steady, linear, predictable, or unidirectional. Here the adage of "one step forward, two steps back" does not apply, though it might feel like it does. The Trajectory Tracker is here to help you in this confusing reality to visualize where you are and where you want to be. Be sure to date a trajectory when you complete it so you can later compare it to others. Hopefully in this way, over time, you will clearly see that you have moved forward overall. If you compare the completed trackers and find that you have *not* moved forward, consider that an indicator you should reach out for more help.

On the next page you will see an image of a path with three main areas: Start, Middle, and Beyond. *Start* indicates the place or time when your thoughts and actions are stuck in the past, with minimal participation in the present and no thoughts of the future. *Middle* signals a shift to a state where you are living more in the present, able both to remember the past without getting caught up in it and to envision the future. *Beyond* is the final stage of the path where you now fully participate in daily life and actively work on building toward the future. You have learned how to carry your loved one's presence with you as you desire and to control when to reflect and remember.

Considering those three main areas, reflect on where you are in the present moment. Are you close to the start, firmly in the middle, or somewhere between? Place a mark along the pathway, indicating the date, to show where you think you are at this point, and add a few comments or sentences about why you placed yourself there. Then write a goal for where you want to be when you complete the next tracker.

Through

Date:

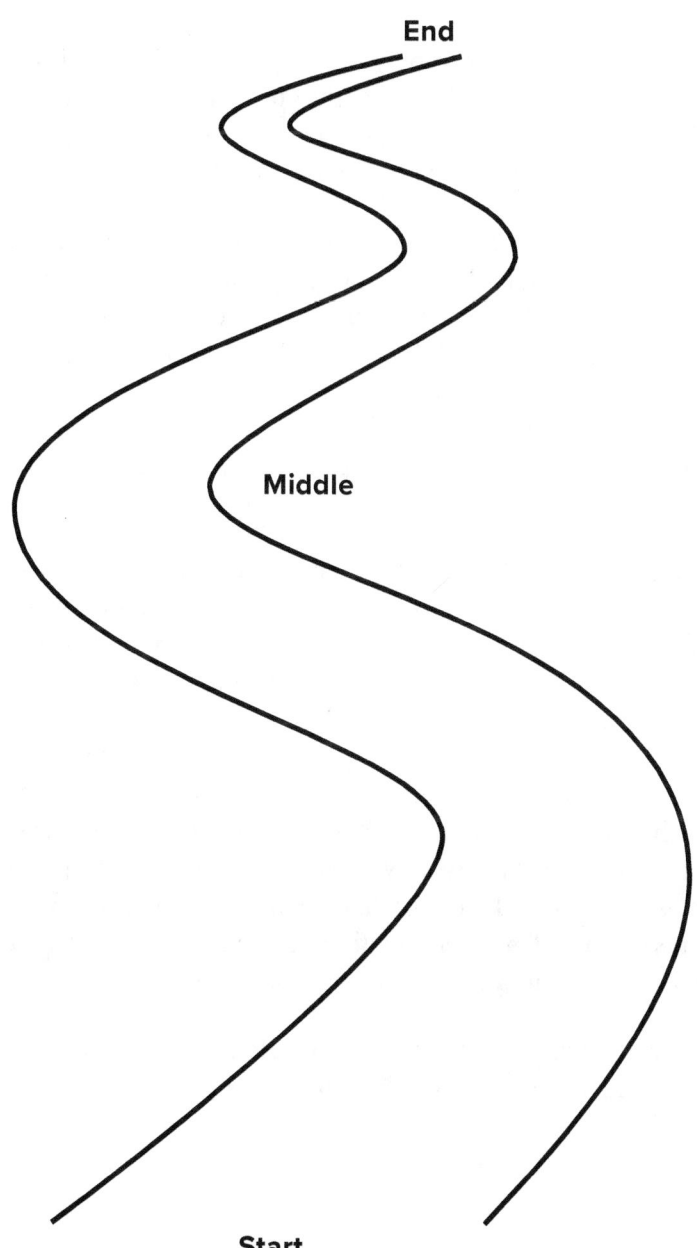

A FINAL TOOLKIT: CLAIMING AN IDENTIFIER

Note: This is meant to be your very last Toolkit, so if you land on this page but the rest of the guide is not yet complete, please work your way through everything else before returning here. I promise it will make sense then!

In grief, "identifiers like 'the griever,' 'grievers,' and 'the bereaved' are used to describe those who are working through grief after the death of a significant person. At some point, though, that identifier no longer fits. What once gave freedom to explore feelings and to take time to adapt now feels almost confining and limiting. Grief changes from being something you are into something you experience as needed."
Faith Doesn't Erase Grief, 190

My hope is that because you have embraced and released emotions, established and let go of connections, rediscovered your identity, and found your through, you are now able to move those grief identifiers mentioned in the quote to the background and lead with something else. Reaching this place is a victory worth celebrating, so take your time to decide what your new identifier is, and then write it loud and proud in the space provided. Use markers, stickers, maybe even glitter; celebrate the work you have done to get to this point! Do so with confidence in what you have learned. No matter where you go from here, neither your person nor your grief will ever be out of reach when you need them.

So, what will it be? Dreamer? Experiencer? Practitioner of Life? Traveler? Conqueror? Fighter? Survivor? Phoenix?

By the way, this is one of those times when I love to hear from readers. See the About the Author page at the end of this guidebook to contact me with your new identifier.

Now What?

When you first sat down with this guidebook, I would guess it was difficult to imagine ever making your way through it. If you're reading these words, though, the likelihood is that you have. Congratulations! Giving such focused attention to your grief takes courage and determination, commitment and stamina. *You* gave yourself the gift of this time, and I hope you recognize that, because you did, you are now better equipped to tend to others as well. So many of us fixate our efforts anywhere but on ourselves when we most need care, but the truth is you cannot give from an empty cup, and grief depletes. All the work you have done throughout this guide, along with any other grief work you've completed, has served to refill your cup.

So, seriously, now what? *Now you live.* You take the identity and purpose you have claimed in these pages and put it to work, and you do so free of fear that you must leave your person behind to do so. You know how to carry them forward with you. You can trust the work you have done, and you can trust the Spirit.

Before you put this book back on the shelf, I have a few

final requests. First, flip back through and ensure you have marked any pages that will benefit you the next time a grief wave strikes. Secondly, find the goal you wrote for your faith life (see page 98–99), and if you haven't already, write it somewhere you will see it every day since you will no longer be looking regularly through these pages. Keep working toward that goal. If you've already met this goal, consider setting a new one.

Third, choose one or two things from this guidebook that you can share with someone when they tell you that year two is harder than year one. How can you encourage them to dive into their own grief work? Fourth, keep this guidebook easily accessible. If you need this kind of support in the future, don't hesitate to take this book back out and comb through any section that seems newly helpful or interesting to you. What you do and learn and think the next time around will not be identical to this time through, so the book still has a purpose to serve. If you previously wrote within the spaces provided, just use a separate journal or notebook to track your Toolkit responses and Action Challenges.

Finally, add "educator" to your list of identifiers. People deserve to know that faith truly does not erase grief and also that faith can inform grief. People deserve to know that they can, with work, move forward from where they are on day one. I'll keep shouting it from the rooftops, but imagine the validation and affirmation we could give others if you joined me!

Be well, friend. Reach out through my social media or contact page (see my About the Author information at the end of this guidebook). If this guidebook was helpful, let someone know. I'm proud of you for sticking it out. Well done, good and faithful child of God!

About the Author

Kate J. Meyer, MDiv, LPC, is a speaker, ordained minister, and licensed professional counselor who has worked with people as their chaplain or grief counselor in both private practice and hospice care. The majority of her time is spent working with the bereaved as they navigate grief and faith. Kate's background, education, and practice create a fulcrum balancing both the theology and psychology of grief. Kate is also the author of *The Red Couch* and *The Yellow Dress*. Visit katejmeyer.com to sign up for her newsletter, follow her on social media, or contact Kate directly there as well.

About Lake Drive Books

Lake Drive Books is an independent publishing company offering books that help you heal, grow, and discover. We champion books about values and strategies, not ideologies, and authors who are spiritually rich, contextually intelligent, and focused on human flourishing. We want to help readers feel seen.

If you like this or any of our other books at lakedrivebooks.com, we could use your help: please follow our authors on social media, subscribe to their newsletters, and tell others what you think of their remarkable books.

Also from Kate J. Meyer

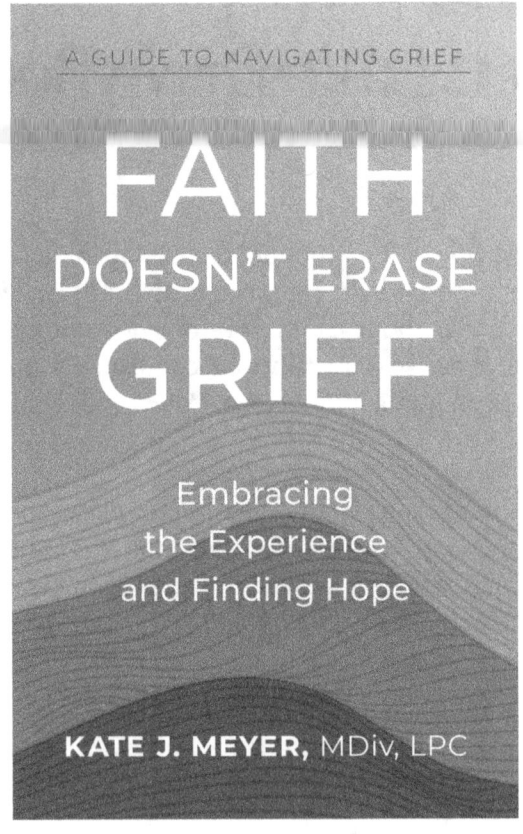

www.ingramcontent.com/pod-product-compliance
Lightning Source LLC
LaVergne TN
LVHW012042070526
838202LV00056B/5568